SKETCH MAP O
MIDLAND ROUTE
DERBY TO MANCHESTER

All station names shown are the original ones.

NOT TO SCALE

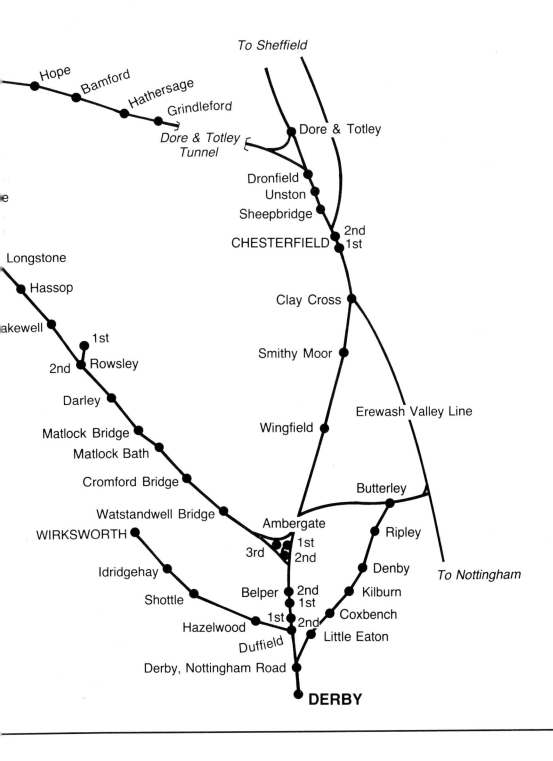

To Sheffield

Hope
Bamford
Hathersage
Grindleford
Dore & Totley Tunnel
Dore & Totley
Dronfield
Unston
Sheepbridge
CHESTERFIELD 2nd 1st
Clay Cross
Longstone
Hassop
akewell
1st
2nd
Rowsley
Darley
Matlock Bridge
Matlock Bath
Cromford Bridge
Smithy Moor
Erewash Valley Line
Wingfield
Watstandwell Bridge
WIRKSWORTH
Butterley
Ambergate
Ripley
1st
3rd
2nd
Idridgehay
Denby
To Nottingham
Shottle
Belper 2nd
1st
Kilburn
1st 2nd
Coxbench
Hazelwood
Little Eaton
Duffield
Derby, Nottingham Road
DERBY

MIDLAND
THROUGH
THE PEAK

Abbreviations used in this book

BR	British Railways	MCR	Midland Counties Railway
CLC	Cheshire Lines Committee	MNM&HJR	Marple, New Mills & Hayfield Junction Railway
GN&NS Jt.	Great Northern and North Staffordshire Joint Committee	MR	Midland Railway
GNR	Great Northern Railway	MS&LR	Manchester, Sheffield & Lincolnshire Railway
L&YR	Lancashire & Yorkshire Railway	MSJ&AR	Manchester South Junction & Altrincham Railway
LD&ECR	Lancashire, Derbyshire & East Coast Railway	NMR	North Midland Railway
LMSR	London, Midland & Scottish Railway	SA&MR	Sheffield, Ashton & Manchester Railway
LNWR	London & North Western Railway	S&MC	Sheffield & Midland Committee
M&BR	Manchester & Birmingham Railway	S&WJR	Stockport & Woodley Junction Railway
MBM&MJR	Manchester, Buxton, Matlock & Midlands Junction Railway	ST&AJR	Stockport, Timperley & Altrincham Junction Railway

MIDLAND THROUGH THE PEAK

A pictorial history of the Midland Railway
main line routes between
Derby and Manchester

BRIAN RADFORD

Unicorn Books

This book is dedicated to my parents

THE AUTHOR

Brian Radford comes from a railway family and in his youth engaged in the pastime of 'train spotting' which grew into a love of railways, and in particular the old Midland Railway.

After an engineering apprenticeship in the Derby Locomotive Works he moved into the Locomotive Drawing Office at Derby in time to make a small contribution, at a very junior level, to the last few years of work on BR Standard locomotives before diesel locomotives took the centre of the stage.

At present he is a Project Engineer in the DM&EE Department (BRB) at the Railway Technical Centre involved in the refurbishment of coaching stock.

His other interests include music, opera singing and local history, and he is the vice-chairman and acquisitions officer of the Midland Railway Trust Ltd, which is devoted to the creation of a major museum dedicated to the Midland in Derbyshire and which, as a microcosm of the Midland, will reflect many of the scenes in this book.

Front cover illustration
Midland 2-4-0 102 stands at the head of a train of Midland clerestory coaches in Chee Dale in typical Peak scenery about 1900. (B.R., L.M.R.)

First published in 1988 by
UNICORN BOOKS,
16 Laxton Gardens,
Paddock Wood,
Kent

© J. B. Radford 1988

ISBN 1 85241 001 9
401276

Typeset by Vitaset, Paddock Wood.
Printed by Biddles Ltd
Guildford and King's Lynn.

ACKNOWLEDGEMENTS

I wish to place on record my grateful thanks to all those friends, individuals and organisations who generously agreed to the loan of photographs and other material for use in this book. Special thanks to Vic Forster and David Tee, both of whom devoted more time than I could reasonably expect to reading the manuscript, correcting errors and omissions, revising and making helpful suggestions and who also placed their own photographic collections at my disposal. I also record my thanks to Eddie Roberts for assistance with material from the Manchester area and to Janet Baker who prepared the typescript from my, at times, barely legible manuscript.

The text is drawn from personal observations and a number of printed sources principally the following: *Our Iron Roads* and *The Midland Railway – Its Rise and Progress*, both by F. S. Williams; *Clinker's Register of Closed Passenger Stations and Goods Depots; Great Central*, Vols. I - III, by George Dow; *The Peak Line* by John M. Stephenson; *The History of the Midland Railway* by C. E. Stretton; *The Mancunian*, the journal of the Manchester Locomotive Society; and various Midland Railway minutes, documents and timetables.

Finally, my thanks to my wife and family for leaving me undisturbed during the period in which this book was being prepared.

Brian Radford
August 1986

CREDITS

The author gratefully acknowledges the following individuals and organisations who have willingly supplied illustrations and given permission for them to appear in this book. Without their co-operation the various locations and subjects could not have been so well covered.

The numbers quoted refer to page numbers and the prefix letters indicate the position on the page thus: T = Top, C = Centre, B = Bottom.

Author and author's collection: 7, 8, 13T, 13C, 19B, 20C, 20B (left), 21T, 21B, 23B (left), 30C, 31T, 32B, 33C, 34T, 35T, 39T, 46T, 47T, 47C, 51T, 51B, 52C, 53C, 54T, 54C, 56C, 56B, 57C, 57B (left & right), 58T, 60T (left & right), 63C, 63B (left), 64C, 64T, 67C, 69T (left & right), 70C, 70B, 71C, 71B, 72C, 72B, 73T, 74T, 78T, 79B, 80T (left & right), 81C, 81B, 82T, 82B, 84C, 86T, 87T, 87C, 87B, 91C, 91B, 92T (right), 95T, 96B, 104B, 105T, 108T (left & right), 108C, 108B, 109C, 110T, C & B, 112C, 113C, 114C, 115B, 116T & C, 118T & C, 119B, 120T, C & B, 122T, 123T, C & B, 124T, 126T (left), 126B, 131C, 132B, 136B, 138B, 140C, 141T (right), 141B. V.R. Anderson: 47B, 48C, 106C, 128C, 135B, 138C. J.M. Bentley collection: 68C. Harold D. Bowtell (courtesy D.F. Tee): 139B. British Rail (LMR): 15T. British Rail/OPC: 59T (right), 78C, 93B, 112T (right), 143T. B.W. Brookbank (courtesy V. Forster): 44B, 45T, 79T, 80B, 98T. W.A. Brown: 134C. E.D. Brunton: 49B. R.J. Buckley: 11C, 16C, 19C, 32T. F.G. Carrier: 9, 16T, 20T (courtesy V. Forster), 62B, 77, 93T, 97B. Oliver Carter collection: 22T, 25T, 31C, 36B, 40C, 104T, 113T, 133B, 137C, 137B. H.C. Casserley: 14C, 15B, 34C, 63B (right), 82C, 83B, 85B, 94T. Clay Cross Co Ltd: 28T, 35C, 35B, 37B. J.A.G.H. Coltas: 122C. J. Cupit (courtesy V. Forster): 37B, 72T. Derby Museums: 25C, 26C, 29B, 49C, 62C, 117C & B, 129B (left), 130T (right), 131T, 138T, 139C, 141C. Derbyshire Library Service: 18B, 20B (right), 23B (right). M.W. Earley: 88B, 89T. J.A. Fleming (Midland Railway Trust Archives): 11B, 12C, 44C, 67B, 73C, 73B, 75T, 75C, 80C, 86B. V. Forster: 14B, 23T, 32C, 36C, 38C, 62T, 63T, 66C, 68B, 71T, 74B, 83C, 90B, 92B, 95B, 100T, 103C, 124B, 127B, 143C. G. Fox (courtesy V.R. Anderson): 106T. A.C. Gilbert (courtesy V. Forster): 94B. A.C. Gilbert (courtesy D.F. Tee): 116B.

W.L. Good: 12T. B.K.B. Green (courtesy V. Forster): 60B, 93C, 103T, 109T, 132C, 135T. Andrew Handyside & Co Ltd (Author's Collection): 142C. C.B. Harley (courtesy V. Forster): 100B. J.F. Henton (courtesy V. Forster): 31B. T.G. Hepburn (courtesy V. Forster): 10C, 41C, 85C. W.H. Hewitt: 48B. S.K. Huson: 10B. D. Ibbotson: 59T (left). Richard Keene, Derby: 18T. M.L. Knighton collection: 24B, 74C, 79C, 81T, 99T (courtesy D.F. Tee) 99C, 102C, 105B. Lens of Sutton: 37T, 58C, 59C. Tom Lewis (courtesy D.F. Tee & Mrs Lewis): 95C, 98B, 129T, 129B (right), 130T (left), 133C, 134T, 135C. Lillywhite Ltd: 21C. L.&.G.R.P: 29C, 49T, 51C, 131B. L.M.&.S.R Official (Author's collection): 13B. Locomotive Publishing Company: 17T. London & North Western Railway Co Official (Author's collection): 66T, 114B. Manchester Libraries: 140T, 142T. Markham & Company Ltd: 42B. George Marsden & Son: 18C. M. Mensing: 88T. Midland Railway Official (Author's Collection): 10T, 12B, 13B, 15C, 19T, 22C, 24C, 25B, 26T, 27, 29T, 33T, 39C, 39B, 40B, 42T, 43, 45B, 50T, 52C, 52B, 60C, 61, 65T, C & B, 66B, 67T, 69B, 70T, 75B, 76T, 76B, 78B, 84B, 85T, 86C, 89C, 89B, 90T, 101, 128T, 141T (left), 143B. Midland Railway Official (courtesy D.F. Tee): 99B. Midland Railway Trust Archives: 16B, 22B (courtesy M.L. Knighton), 38T, 41T, 64B, 99B. C.H. Nadin: 38B, 40T (courtesy Chesterfield Library): 42C, 44T. National Railway Museum (Midland Railway Official) Crown Copyright: 11T, 46C, 46B, 50B, 56T, 68T, 115T, 115C, 127C, 130B. R.B. Parr (courtesy V. Forster): 26B. H.J. Patterson Rutherford: 54B. H.B. Priestley: 33B, 37C, 45C, 48T, 53B, 55C, 55B, 94C, 96C. Real Photographs Co Ltd: 17C, 17B, 23C, 30T, 83T, 92T (left), 92C, 102T, 103B, 140B, 142B. A. Rimmer: 28C. Royal Commission on the Historical Monuments of England: 28B, 53T, 55T, 57T, 91T, 118B. W.H. Smith: 41B. Stockport M.B. Libraries: 107B, 125T, C&B, 126T (right), 126C, 128B, 129C, 134B. D.F. Tee & D.F. Tee collection: 52T, 58B, 59C, 59B, 84T, 90C, 96T, 97T, 97C, 98C, 100C, 102B, 106B, 107C, 109T, 111T, C&B, 112T (left), 112B, 114T, 119T, 119C, 121T, C&B, 122B, 130C, 132T, 133T, 136T, 136C, 137T, 139T. J. Valentine & Sons, Dundee: 14T, 24T, 34T, 36T, 104C, 105C, 113B, 117T, 127T. V.R. Webster: 30B.

Contents

Matlock Bath

From Matlock Bath's half-timbered station
   I see the black dissenting spire –
Thin witness of a congregation,
   Stone emblem of a Handel choir;
In blest Bethesda's limpid pool
Comes treacling out of Sunday School.

By cool Siloam's shady rill –
   The sounds are sweet as strawberry jam:
I raise mine eyes unto the hill,
   The beetling HEIGHTS OF ABRAHAM;
The branchy trees are white with rime
In Matlock Bath this winter-time,

And from the whiteness, grey uprearing,
   Huge cliffs hang sunless ere they fall,
A tossed and stony ocean nearing
   The moment to o'erwhelm us all:
Eternal Father, strong to save,
How long wilt thou suspend the wave?

How long before the pleasant acres
   Of intersecting LOVERS' WALKS
Are rolled across by limestone breakers,
   Whole woodlands snapp'd like cabbage stalks?
O God, our help in ages past,
How long will SPEEDWELL CAVERN last?

In this dark dale I hear the thunder
   Of houses folding with the shocks,
The GRAND PAVILION buckling under
   The weight of the ROMANTIC ROCKS,
The hardest Blue John ash-trays seem
To melt away in thermal steam.

Deep in their Nonconformist setting
   The shivering children wait their doom –
The father's whip, the mother's petting
   In many a coffee-coloured room;
And attic bedrooms shriek with fright,
For dread of *Pilgrims of the Night.*

Perhaps it's this that makes me shiver
   As I ascend the slippery path
High, high above the sliding river
   And terraces of Matlock Bath:
A sense of doom, a dread to see
The *Rock of Ages cleft for me.*

The late *Sir John Betjeman*
(from 'High and Low')

*(Reproduced by kind permission
of John Murray Ltd.)*

Introduction

Above
The five arches, a railway bridge over the Derwent, with a North Midland Railway train approaching Derby Station in 1840.

Of the three original companies which were combined on 10 May 1844 to form the Midland Railway Company, the North Midland had by far the most difficult line of route from Derby via Ambergate, Chesterfield, Masborough, Cudworth and Normanton, to their northernmost station at Leeds.

Three years after the memorable meeting of coal owners at the Sun Inn, Eastwood, on 16 August 1832 which led to the eventual building of the Midland Counties Railway, George Stephenson and his secretary, Charles Binns, set off in a yellow post chaise up the Duffield Road from Derby on a beautiful autumnal morning to find the best route for the new 72-mile line. Eventually George chose the valley route, raising the level of the line only sufficiently from the floor of the valleys to avoid flooding and setting a limit to the gradients of 1 in 330 or sixteen feet per mile, this only being exceeded for a short distance on the approach to Clay Cross Tunnel from the south. Mineral traffic was intended to be the mainstay of the line and those towns not directly on his valley route had to be satisfied with branch lines!

Frederick Swanwick, the Assistant and Resident Engineer appointed on 23 September 1836, had to overcome many obstacles put into his path; not least of these were 'watchers' placed by the gentry to guard private estates. He overcame the latter by surveying at night and astonished Sir William Pilkington, who had been particularly obstructive south-east of Wakefield, by producing a detailed survey of the honourable gentleman's estate which matched his own private survey kept under lock and key and thought to be the only one in existence!

Lord Wharncliffe supported Charles Vignoles in his assertion that the line should run from Chesterfield directly through to Sheffield which would have involved considerable earthworks, cuttings and embankments in excess of ninety feet, but pressure from this quarter was overcome. The solution adopted for that city was a short line some 5½ miles long, to be called the Sheffield and Rotherham Railway which joined the North Midland at Masborough. Further opposition came from the Aire and Calder Navigation which was only withdrawn after the line of route was changed by a deviation, some 2 miles 36 chains long, carrying the railway across Hunslet Moor, well away from the south bank of the River Aire, on the final approaches to Leeds.

Thus the North Midland Bill received Royal Assent on 4 July 1836 and by the beginning of 1837 work was already in hand. Twenty-eight contracts were involved, including seven tunnels, the longest being Clay Cross at 1,760 yards which formed part of Contract No. 8, and the construction of more than 200 bridges. By the summer of 1838 the Derby end was the scene of great activity, the Nottingham turnpike having been lowered and the approaches to the new trijunct station at Derby was laid out with its goods and engine sheds, workshops and offices. Milford tunnel was in course of construction; at Wingfield 350,000cu yd of earthworks being excavated, whilst at Clay Cross 400 yards of the tunnel were complete, with six fifteen-horse whinseys at work at six vertical shafts from which men were working in opposite directions on twelve faces at once, quite apart from

Above
Derby station in 1840 showing the three-bay train shed and a North Midland Railway locomotive about to back onto a train. The train on the extreme right in the train shed is in the Midland Counties Railway bay platform.

work at the ends.

Quite the most spectacular set of workings were at Bull Bridge just beyond Ambergate where the line was to pass underneath the Cromford Canal, which was to be carried on an aqueduct, and then immediately over the River Amber. The two summits of the line were at the southern end of Clay Cross tunnel, 360 feet above sea level, and at Royston some 200 feet.

The opening of the North Midland line took place in two sections. On 11 May 1840 through carriages from the Sheffield & Rotherham Company's 5.30am service from Wicker station, Sheffield, were attached to the North Midland's first 'up' train at Masborough.

Traffic was heavier than expected and by the time the train reached Chesterfield it was already sixty-five minutes late. Here George Stephenson and George Hudson, his guest at Tapton House, joined the train which ran, with pilot engine assistance at the rear, to the north end of Clay Cross tunnel where the pilot engine was detached. However the rails were wet and three-quarters of the way through the tunnel the train slipped to a standstill, whereupon a man was sent back on foot to fetch the pilot engine. Passengers at the rear of the train, fearing a collision, climbed out into the tunnel, and began wandering about in the darkness. Order was restored only by George Stephenson's broad Northumbrian accent, clearly heard above the din, complaining of this mismanagement and forcefully urging people to rejoin the train.

Because of these delays it was not until 9.30am that the train eventually reached Derby, one hour and forty-five minutes late.

However the first 'down' train, comprising four First and four Second Class coaches hauled by two locomotives and with Robert Stephenson on the footplate of the pilot engine, left on time at 9.15am and reached Masborough on schedule although the Sheffield passengers arrived twenty-four minutes late.

Completion of the North Midland line into the Hunslet Lane passenger station at Leeds was delayed by a few weeks and the whole line was officially opened on 30 June 1840. A special train of thirty-four First and Second Class coaches left Leeds at 8.03am and was joined at Normanton by a number of carriages from the York and North Midland Railway containing George Hudson and directors and officials of that line, with a further carriage containing directors of the then un-opened Manchester and Leeds Railway. The company was further swelled at Masborough by the addition of further vehicles from the Sheffield & Rotherham through service to Derby, so that the total number of vehicles reached sixty-two! Clearly, it was necessary to split the train and it was worked forward to Derby in two portions, each hauled by two loco-motives with a pilot engine at the rear.

Bands played on the platforms at Cudworth, Chesterfield and Belper and at Derby the guests tucked into a 'cold collation' with wine, served on the platform, while a further band

Above
Derby station in 1840 showing the three-bay train shed and a North Midland Railway locomotive about to back onto a train. The train on the extreme right in the train shed is in the Midland Counties Railway bay platform.

played 'martial and other suitable airs'. Two enormous tables stretched along the platform but sitting was out of the question. The new station was tastefully decorated with evergreens for the occasion. A return train left for Leeds at 2.30pm and conveyed about 500 guests, arriving there at 6.55pm.

That same evening the North Midland directors entertained their guests to a dinner at the Music Hall in Albion Street, Derby. 'Several hundred ladies' attended the event with George Carr Glyn, the chairman of the Company, presiding and later in the evening guests were conveyed home to York and Sheffield by special trains which left Derby at 10.30pm.

Public traffic began the next day, and so ended the opening chapter in the story of the first vital midlands link from Derby to the north.

Over the 72-mile route there were 200 bridges, 7 tunnels, totalling 2½ miles in length, and 26 stations; costing in all 3 million pounds. At the height of construction 10,000 men from all parts of the country had been employed on the works under a number of contractors.

Thus was opened the first part of the eventual route which led the Midland Railway through the Peak to Manchester and beyond, as our story will tell.

1
Rails
to the North

Leaving Derby station the line immediately passes over the former Derby canal and the Five Arches railway bridge which originally carried both the North Midland and Midland Counties lines over the River Derwent. The original Midland Counties line curved away to the east immediately beyond the bridge and proceeded via Chaddesden on its way to Nottingham and Leicester.

The Five Arches bridge was the location for one of the three ticket platforms where trains were held for the examination of tickets before entering the Derby station, which for more than a century was an 'open' one except on Sundays. It has recently been reinstated as a 'open' station, Sundays included.

One Derby station character had a lucky escape on this very bridge, as recalled by G. J. Pratt in his *Midland Railway Memories*. He was Robert Bartlett, the tall policeman who 'looked after things' at the front of the station, hence his nick-name 'Hall Door Bob'. One windy night, after a visit to Nottingham, he got out of the train when it reached the ticket platform and fell – or was blown – off the parapet of the bridge into the dangerous waters of the river below. He was somehow rescued, but Pratt recalls that Bartlett was never quite the same man again.

Beyond the Five Arches bridge lay the Midland's own signal works which began in quite a small way with a mere dozen or so carpenters, fitters and smiths and grew by the early 1880s to a department employing some 500 men at Derby with another 300 elsewhere on the system.

Previous page
Former Midland 2-4-0 179 pilots an LMS Compound 4-4-0 1090 on a 'down' express through Duffield *c*1927.

Top
Derby station en fete for the Royal Show, June 1906, which was visited by King Edward VII.

Centre
LMS compound 4-4-0 leaving Derby with the 4.10pm to Manchester Central, 11 July 1959.

Bottom
45618 *New Hebrides* of Derby shed makes a spirited start from Derby station with a winter's afternoon train for Manchester in 1960.

Top
The Midland signal gantries at the north end of Derby station in February 1905, looking north.

Centre
Ex-Midland 4-4-0 40520 of Rowsley shed leaves Derby with the 5.07pm stopping train for Darley Dale, 22 June 1950.

Bottom
'Royal Scot' Class 4-6-0 46116 *Irish Guardsman* passes over the five arches bridge at Derby with a relief Bristol to Sheffield express in the 1950s.

For convenience the signal department was split into twenty or so districts, each overlooked by its own inspector, with between fifteen and twenty assistants.

The tallest signal posts of Midland times measured 65 feet in length, of which 6 feet was buried in the ground, and were supported by wires attached to the top, whilst a normal signal measured 45 or 50 feet. Made of squared section Memel pine, a resinous wood resistant to rotting, the posts tapered from 14 inches square at the bottom to 8 inches square at the top, and 1,200 or so such posts were supplied for use on the Midland system each year.

However, equally important were the signalboxes with their lever frames and other equipment such as block signalling indicators, bells, repeaters, etc. Every part of an installation, from the box side and roof panels to the complex individual parts of the frames, levers, bedplates, interlocking

etc, was made in these works which had extensive machine shops to facilitate manufacture. The lines connecting Derby Junction and Derby North Junction on the main line to the north, and Derby South Junction on the direct line avoiding Derby via Chaddesen Sidings, formed a triangle, the centre of which was used as a timber and equipment storage area. Access was by means of an under-bridge and a narrow-gauge railway system to the main works, which stood to the left of the line on a site now occupied by the new premises of the *Derby Evening Telegraph*.

Just beyond Derby North Junction, the site of which is now a part of Derby's new inner ring-road system, the line formerly crossed both the Derby Canal and the Nottingham Road and proceeded into Derby Nottingham Road station (128 miles 49 chains from St Pancras). Closed completely on 6 March 1967 the station, which opened on 1 September 1856, was built to serve the local area and also provided a service to Derby Racecourse where meetings were held in March, September and November until they ceased about 1938. Before 1852 horse racing was held on a course in The Siddals near the station. County cricket matches are now played on this ground by the Derbyshire County Cricket Club, founded in November 1870, which uses the main grandstand as its cricket pavilion, whilst the remaining exten-sive area is used for amateur football and cricket activities in season.

Just north, on the west side, lies the extensive St Mary's Goods depot, the main inward receiving and despatch point for the Midland, and in former times a hive of industry as manufac-tured goods and raw materials arrived in the town or left for journeys to all points of the compass.

Hard by lies Little Chester, the Roman campsite where an important

Top
'Deeley' 0-6-4 tank 2019 entering Derby from the north over the five arches bridge with a Nottingham to Derby local which has run via Chaddesden sidings in June 1925.

Centre
'Jubilee' 4-6-0 45699 *Galatea* runs into Derby with a Newcastle to Bristol train. The curve to Chaddesden sidings can be seen on the right.

Bottom
Derby cattle docks, just north of the station, 26 November 1909, looking north.

settlement, situated at a focal point of the roads from Chester, Buxton, Wirksworth and Sawley, and lying on Ryknield Street on its way from Bath to Yorkshire, was established around the year AD 80. A fort was constructed and strategically placed at this point to control a ford across the River Derwent, and continued in use until around AD 370.

The Midland line passed under the Great Northern Railway's line from Grantham and Nottingham to that company's station in Friargate, Derby, constructed with great difficulty since it approached the town from the east on a high curving viaduct which spanned several roads, the Midland's own main line and the River Derwent. The GNR line opened for passenger traffic on 1 April 1878 in an attempt to compete for traffic in the south of Derbyshire and in Staffordshire but it

Top
A fine engraving of the Nottingham Road at Derby with the railway crossing both the road and the Derby canal. To the right, at the end of the set of bridges, a station was provided at a later date.

Centre
Derby's Nottingham Road station in 1906 decorated for the Royal Show.

Bottom
Midland 0-6-0 3440 on a train conveying 100 tons of machinery parts leaving Derby St Mary's goods yard, 24 October 1935.

was never a serious threat to Midland supremacy in the area, although it had a useful liaison with the North Staffordshire Railway at Egginton Junction. It closed to passengers on 7 September 1964, and completely as from 4 September 1967.

Continuing northwards the line passes the site of Breadsall level-crossing, which once afforded a route from Allestree and Darley Abbey on the west side to the main road from Derby between Breadsall and Little Eaton. A new dual-carriageway portion of the A38 trunk route now sweeps over the line here, where the North Midland planned, but never built, a three-arch bridge.

The slender spire of Breadsall Church, dedicated to All Saints, can be seen to the east of the line, and one is reminded that the church was burned out on 4 June 1914, allegedly set alight by women suffragettes in an attempt to secure the franchise for

their sex. Nearby is Breadsall Priory, a Jacobean house built on the remains of the original Breadsall Priory which dated back to the early 1260s and was founded by the Austin Friars, and later much enlarged. Breadsall is a pleasant village which originally had its own station on the Great Northern Line, and up to the present day it has escaped the scourge of modern housing development.

To the left lies the ancient village of Darley Abbey, seat of the Austin Canons who moved here early in the reign of Henry II, and in later years the site of a large cotton mill established by the Evans family in 1783. The roadway across the weir over the river Derwent was until recently subject to tolls payable at the toll-house on the east bank.

Slightly to the north lies the old village of Allestree, and the nearby Allestree Park with a private residence, built by the same Evans family; both house and park now provide amenities for the public, and both villages have been encircled by modern housing estates.

On the right at this point is the branch railway which once ran through Little Eaton to Ripley and on to meet the Ambergate to Pye Bridge line just west of Butterley. This served the villages of Coxbench, Kilburn and Denby with their coal-mining interests. These mining villages mark a distinctive change in local accent, and from here northwards the broad Derbyshire

Top
Breadsall church and post office.

Centre
An 'up' Wirksworth branch train at Breadsall Crossing near Derby, 25 June 1941, with ex-Midland 0-4-4T 1408 in charge of a pair of ex-Midland clerestory carriages.

Bottom
Ex-Midland 4-4-0 443 at Breadsall crossing with a heavy 'down' express passing a fine gantry of Midland signals whilst a double-headed freight train approaches on the goods lines.

dialect is very marked. Phrases like 'Wor ee wee issen?' and 'Ay enyy onya ottya?' give a flavour, roughly translated as 'Was he unaccompanied?' and 'Have any of you hurt yourselves?'. This type of dialect extends, and becomes even broader, the whole way up the Erewash Valley to Chesterfield and beyond, and persists strongly even in these days of mass communication.

Little Eaton had an earlier railway before the Midland in its gang-road, built mainly to carry coal but also stone, pottery and 'clogs of wood'. Opened on 11 May 1795 it ran from Little Eaton Wharf, situated on an arm of the Derby canal, to Smithy Houses some 4¾ miles away. On this gang-road horses were used singly or in teams to haul containers of coal, etc on four-wheeled trucks from the pits to the canal wharf, where the complete container and contents were lifted off by crane and lowered into the barges – an early use of container traffic! The line closed in July 1908 having remained largely unaltered for the whole of its existence.

Back on our northward route, having passed over the Derwent, the railway arrives at Duffield (133 miles 8 chains) where the Wirksworth branch leaves the main line on the left. This branch had a curious development for it was originally built to be part of the Midland route to Manchester, since at that time the company was

Top
A Ripley branch passenger train at Little Eaton station, 31 December 1915. Note the Midland gradient post on the right.

Centre
Remains of Little Eaton gangroad at the wharf alongside the Derby canal. The coals etc were carried in containers which were off-loaded directly into canal barges.

Bottom
Midland 0-4-4T 1365 entering Ripley station with a local train in June 1926. Passenger traffic ceased 1 June 1930.

frustrated by the London & North Western Railway Company's determination to prevent that city being reached by the Midland. The L&NWR and Midland companies had jointly leased a stretch of line between Ambergate and Rowsley, constructed originally by the grandly titled 'Manchester, Buxton, Matlock and Midlands Junction Railway' and opened on 4 June 1849. In fact only that section of line was opened and although the company also purchased the seventeen-mile-long Cromford canal, there were scant prospects of success for such an ambitious project. As we shall later see, the Midland took a new alignment at Rowsley and commenced building lines to Buxton and New Mills, by Acts of 1860 and 1862 respectively.

Since the LNWR could have frustrated the Midland's aim to run over their jointly-leased line between Ambergate and Rowsley, a new branch line was established to take the Midland via Wirksworth to join up with the High Peak Railway and, if necessary later, their new lines north of Rowsley. The station at Duffield was re-sited a short distance to the south adjacent to the new Wirksworth branch platform, and the new branch line, which follows the Ecclesbourne Valley, was opened on 1 October 1867 with intermediate stations at Hazelwood, Shottle and Idridgehay. The passenger-train service was never particularly frequent, there being a mere four or five trains each way on weekdays and one on Sunday afternoons to Derby

Top
Veteran double-framed Kirtley 0-6-0 2498 passing Duffield church with a northbound freight train *c*1929.

Centre
LMS 2-6-2T 1206 approaching the branch platform at Duffield with a train from Wirksworth, 7 June 1947.

Bottom
The stationmaster and his family are posed on the platform of Hazelwood station on the Wirksworth branch in this delightful period scene before the turn of the century.

and return. This was augmented for a time in 1906 by an additional auto-car train in mid-morning after Wirksworth's inhabitants had agitated for an improved service.

The line was never constructed beyond Wirksworth for the LNWR opposition eventually ceased and the Midland purchased the Ambergate to Rowsley line outright on 1 July 1871.

Wirksworth is a characteristic Peak-town, built mostly of Derbyshire stone, with a history steeped in lead mining dating back to Roman and Saxon times, whilst its modern industries are largely bound up with the extensive limestone quarries which encircle it to the north.

Wirksworth provided the setting for George Eliot's novel *Adam Bede* and her aunt, Elizabeth Evans, whose memorial is in the Methodist Chapel, was the model for Dinah Morris, Bede's wife. The cottage where Elizabeth Evans and her husband lived still stands a mile from the town opposite the tape mill where he was Manager.

The 1,000-year-old Wirksworth church has a unique sculptured and figured Saxon coffin stone and a large font over 700 years old. This charming town still keeps its annual festival of well dressing at Whitsuntide in thanksgiving for the gift of water, and several former wells and taps in the town are decorated with magnificent wooden-framed clay panels, some up to two metres high, into which are presssed flower petals and foliage of

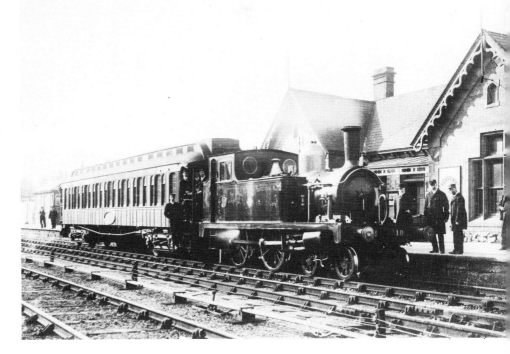

Top
Wirksworth station, looking north.

Centre
Autocar train at Wirksworth in 1906 comprising Midland and Great Northern 4-4-0 tank No. 10, then on loan to the Midland, with ex-Pullman parlour car 'Minerva' serving as trailer.

Bottom
Wirksworth branch platform at Duffield, with main line platforms to the right.

all kinds to build up the chosen picture illustrating some Biblical text or similar theme. The modern revival of this ancient custom dated back to the year 1827 when piped water first arrived.

The branch from Duffield to Wirksworth was temporarily closed to passengers on 16 June 1947 and finally from 1 January 1949, and goods traffic ceased on 1 April 1968, although the branch remains open for mineral traffic and considerable, though decreasing, quantities of stone are still moved.

Duffield is an ancient village and in Norman times was the main approach to Duffield Frith, a Royal Forest some thirty miles in circumference and stocked with deer. It has a Norman church dating back to the twelfth century and dedicated to St Alkmund. On Castle Hill the de Ferrers family, Earls of Derby, built an enormous stone keep, nearly 100 feet square with walls 16 feet thick and second only in size to the Tower of London. This keep was destroyed in the year 1266 when Earl Ferrers was attainted for treason and the stone was used to build the river bridge and extend the church. The few remaining traces of the keep are National Trust property.

The village was once a centre for country crafts but the arrival of the railway and the industrial revolution caused these to decline. Today attractive modern homes are spreading out from its centre, joining with its

Georgian and Victorian town houses in a well-controlled fashion. In the year 1900 it had a population of some 2,000 which has today swelled to nearly 5,000.

Skirting a golf course to the left, the line now proceeds through Milford tunnel (853 yards), which passes through the Chevin hillside. By the summer of 1838 some 168 linear yards had been excavated, and work on the pseudo 'rich Saxon arch' of the north portal had begun, and was completed in time for the line's opening.

Opposite top
Duffield station *c*1910, looking north. The overbridge is a public footpath, and the main station-building houses a ladies' waiting room, stationmaster's office, booking office and, furthest from the camera, the porters' room.

Opposite centre
Town Street, Duffield, looking north *c*1904.

Opposite bottom
Town Street, Duffield, looking towards Derby *c*1895.

Top
Johnson compound 4-4-0 2633 in original condition posed with a train of Midland clerestory stock just south of Milford tunnel, 29 May 1904.

Centre
The 11.30am relief express from London, St Pancras to Leeds passing Duffield, 14 April 1949, behind Stanier Class 5 4-6-0 44757.

Bottom
Interesting engraving depicting the construction of Milford tunnel on the North Midland line in 1839. Note gantry for lifting the tunnel portal stones into position.

Just as the railway emerges from the tunnel, the village of Milford lies to the right, formerly the site of cotton mills erected in 1780 by Jedediah Strutt which, along with houses built for the workers at the foot of steep wooded cliffs, turned this once peaceful hamlet into a thriving industrial centre. The Strutts, along with Richard Arkwright, also developed extensive cotton mills at Belper, our next station. Edward, a son of the family, took the title of Lord Belper in the year 1856 when elevated to the peerage. The family also developed the manufacture of silk and cotton hosiery and this connection continues today with the English Sewing Cotton Company's newest mill which dates back to 1928. Also in the town, Ward, Brettle & Ward at one time turned out more than a hundred-thousand-dozen pairs of stockings in a year.

Top
Midland 0-6-0 2950, from Grimesthorpe shed, on a 'down' goods leaving Milford Tunnel *c*1934.

Centre
Sunny Hill, Milford, looking towards Derby *c*1920.

Bottom
Nailmakers' shop in Joseph Street, Belper

Below
The last Belper nailmaker, Harold Burkinshaw, at work just before the Second World War.

Nail-making became another industry, a trade which had been carried out in earlier years, although on a cottage-industry basis in small nail-makers' shops, one of which survives in Joseph Street. Other manufacturers include adhesives, kitchen ranges and central heating boilers; and Dalton & Co produce reclaimed oils and lubricants under the name of 'Silkolene'.

Belper was much developed under the Strutts, housing of good standard and at reasonable rents being erected, of which Long Row is a good example. The once inconsiderable village became one of the most flourishing market towns in the county, a prosperity to which the coming of the North Midland contributed. Roads were poor and needed improvement by and at the expense of the Strutts and the railway gave a much improved and available means of communication with the outside world. Local Wakes Weeks continued but the 'disgraceful sports of bull-baiting, badger and bear-baiting, cock-fighting and throwing' fell into disuse, although 'cocking and dog-fighting' continued. A population of 8,000 in 1831 swelled to 10,000 by 1841 and by 1900 had grown even higher. Today's population has been swelled by the town becoming a residential dormitory to the city of Derby.

The name of Belper comes from 'Beau Repaire' where Edmund, Earl of Lancaster, who died in 1296 had a hunting lodge and founded a chapel to St John the Baptist. As the railway passes through Belper in a deep cutting, much of the town goes unobserved by the rail traveller. In earlier times this cutting caused severe problems, and after partial collapse it had to be rebuilt. Within the space of one mile no less than twelve bridges carry the streets and lanes of the town over the railway.

Top
Mill workers' houses built by Strutt in Crown Terrace, Belper.

Centre
King Street, Belper. The Midland main line passes beneath this street about half-way to the road junction at the bottom.

Bottom
View of the Midland line in the long cutting as it passes between and beneath Belper's streets. View taken off King Street, looking south from the station.

The original station at Belper was built on a site 54 chains south of the present one and was Italianate in character with a projecting central block, round-headed windows and a parapet roof. It was demolished in November 1878 following the completion of a new two-platformed station built by John Greenwood at a cost of £2,806 2s 11d, work on the building being well in hand by August 1878.

The station was brought into use on 10 March 1878 in advance of the completion of accommodation. Situated nearer the centre of the town (135 miles 53 chains from St Pancras), the new station attracted more traffic. However, the old goods yard adjacent to the original station continued in use, for there was no room for such facilites in the narrow confines of the cutting where the new passenger station had been sited. All of the buildings for that new Belper station have now been demolished.

As the line leaves the northern end of the cutting it passes beneath the main A6 road and crosses Belper Pool, beside the later-developed river gardens, and then the original North Midland line crossed the River Derwent twice by means of two bridges, one of nine spans and the second of eight, each of fifty feet, the construction of which required 200,000 cubic feet of timber. They were later replaced by steel girder bridges resting on stone piers. Here the line is in a wide valley with wooded slopes on each side and the Derwent meandering along its length.

Next, the railway originally passed through Longland tunnel (101 yards) but this was opened out into a cutting in 1928–9. Then it crosses the Derwent to enter Ambergate, situated at the confluence of the Derwent and the Amber rivers which virtually forms the gateway to the Derbyshire Peaks.

This section of line was widened under a contract which lasted from 1928 to 1932. Originally double-track,

Top
Belper's original North Midland station designed by Francis Thompson and demolished in 1878.

Centre
Belper's second station as seen from platform level, looking north, November 1903. Note the carefully tended flower beds and greenhouses.

Bottom
Period scene at Belper as a Derby bound train arrives hauled by a Midland 2-4-0.

the work included uncovering the Longland tunnel and using the stonework and spoil in making embankments towards Broadholme to the south. Shanks & McEwen, a Scottish firm of contractors, carried out the work and the Butterley Company provided ironwork for the new bridge, which was laid alongside the original to carry two extra tracks over the River Derwent and the main road at Ambergate.

Shanks & McEwen imported a gang of mixed Irish and Scottish navvies who were blended with local men taken on for the contract. Private locomotives were brought in to work on the contractor's lines over the top of Longland Tunnel, hauling from the tunnel loaded spoil wagons to be tipped to widen the existing embankment for the extra tracks. Two of these locomotives were *Peterhead*, an 0–6–0 saddle tank built by Manning Wardle & Company in 1898, maker's number 1378; and an ancient 0–4–0 square saddle tank with outside cylinders named *Bonnie Dundee*, which had been rebuilt by Andrew Barclay, Sons & Co Ltd in 1896.

Top
LMS 4-4-0 602 heads an 'up' semi-fast near Belper in 1930.

Centre
Longland tunnel which was demolished in 1931 as part of the Ambergate widening scheme.

Bottom right
Final stages of the removal of Longland tunnel and the creation of the four-track cutting.

Bottom left
A young angler tries his luck in the Derwent at Belper in the shadow of the East and North Mills.

Belper Road, Ambergate

Ambergate South Junction was re-aligned and by virtue of the new four-track approach the severe curves were considerably eased and the signal box re-sited further to the south, the old wooden box of standard Midland design being replaced by a new LMS version on a brick-built base. When the contract was completed the itinerant gang of workers moved to a similar job at Beattock whilst some of the local men joined the LMSR.

Returning to Ambergate, at this point the North Midland was only constructed with difficulty, the biggest problem involving the construction of Hag Wood (later renamed Toadmoor) tunnel (128 yards) cut through an unstable hillside. The solution adopted by Stephenson was to construct the tunnel in an elliptical shape so that it had least 'diameter' in the vertical direction and most resistance at its sides. The pressure was opposed and the tendency to slip down the inclined base of shale, upon which it rested, minimised.

The first Amber Gate station (so named) was constructed a little to the north of this tunnel, between the tunnel and where the eventual North Junction was installed. It was in Jacobean style with mullioned windows, a steeply pitched roof, Dutch gables and a two-storey tower at the centre of the platform side. It was re-named Ambergate from November 1846, although still shown in Midland timetables as 'Amber Gate' until 1852. It was rebuilt on a new site a quarter-of-a-mile to the south of the Toadmoor tunnel between the lines that formed the junction of the North Midland and the west curve linking with the MBM & MJR's line to

Top
Residents of Belper Road, Ambergate, look on with interest as they are 'immortalised in a moment'.

Centre
Immaculate Johnson 4-4-0 332 at Ambergate South Junction (before the widening) heads a train of Midland clerestory coaches still fitted with running boards to assist passengers at stations with low platforms.

Bottom
Road works in progress at Ambergate in April 1931 to permit construction of the second double-track railway overbridge which is being erected above.

Rowsley, and re-opened on 1 June 1863. Sir Joseph Paxton is thought to have been involved in its re-design to an 'A' shape, but it conformed in general style to the original, although enlarged. In this form it remained in use until the new station, situated at the unique triangular junction, was opened on 10 December 1876, thirty chains further to the north on the Manchester line. This third station had platforms on each side of the twin tracks which formed an open triangle,

Top
The original North Midland station at Ambergate designed by Francis Thompson. It was replaced on 10 December 1876 by a second station on a new site, to a similar but enlarged design.

Centre
Station staff at Ambergate *c*1910: *(left to right)* Standing: unknown youth, Jack Young (clerk), Charles Newbould (telegraph clerk), Robert Manners (stationmaster), P. Searles (clerk), unknown. Seated: W. Houghton (porter), Fred Devereaux (porter), Mr Wilkins (foreman), Amos Rowland (signalman), Ernest Allan (porter).

Bottom
Johnson 4-4-0 451 stands at Ambergate South Junction with an express for Derby in the summer of 1911.

serving trains en route from Derby towards Manchester; Derby towards Sheffield; and from Manchester towards the Erewash Valley, as well as the local services to Mansfield via the Ambergate and Pye Bridge line.

The station lost most of its main line services on 6 March 1967 and became an unstaffed halt from 1 January 1968. It has now lost its platforms on all but the Derby–Matlock line, between which points a diesel railcar service runs mainly for commuters, but also provides for hikers and visitors to the Matlocks, referred to later in this book.

The second station buildings remained in use as stores and offices and were eventually demolished in March 1971.

Top
Ambergate station looking south – a photograph taken before the alterations to the south of Ambergate. A branch train for Mansfield stands on the north curve and in the left foreground can be seen the rope-worked incline of Stephenson's mineral railway from Crich.

Centre
Ambergate station and staff: a photograph taken from the footbridge between Platforms 1 and 2, looking north.

Bottom
A multitude of railway elements are combined in this evocative scene at Ambergate in 1961 as 'Royal Scot' Class 4-6-0 46137 *The Prince of Wales' Volunteers (South Lancashire)* waits to depart from Platform 4 for Derby.

2
To the town of the twisted spire

It was at Ambergate that George Stephenson founded his works to burn limestone, using small coal and slack surplus to requirements from his Clay Cross works, which will be mentioned later. Limestone was extracted from the Crich quarries and brought down the hill to Ambergate by means of a self-acting inclined railway with the use of horses on the easier graded sections. This line opened in 1841 and remained a favourite haunt of Stephenson through to his old age. On one occasion he had brought some visitors from his home at Tapton House, Chesterfield, only to find a breakdown in operations. The party walked along the line, and scarcely had they reached the bottom when loaded wagons at the top broke free and rushed down the slope to smash to pieces at its foot, Stephenson's guests scattering in all directions. As the dust cleared Robert Stephenson and George Carr Glyn peeped cautiously over a wall where they had sought shelter, to be greeted by George's amazed face peering from behind a tree. Both burst into laughter only to be admonished 'Ye dinna need to laugh – tis a hundred pounds out of my way'! Although Stephenson Snr died at Tapton House on 12 August 1848 his quarries at Crich continued to supply good quality limestone to the Clay Cross Works for another 109 years, a total quantity of 6 million tons, all of which travelled down this narrow-gauge line.

The second tramroad at Crich was even older, being built by the Butterley Company in 1793 and continuing in use until 1944. This gang-road carried limestone from Crich quarries to the Amber Wharf on the Cromford canal from where most of it was shipped by barge to the Butterley Company's kilns at Codnor Park, whilst part was turned into lime at a plant at Bull Bridge, near to the Midland main line.

Previous page
Johnson 4-4-0 333 heads south from Chesterfield in 1911 with an express train which includes two horse-boxes.

Top
The Ambergate lime works created by George Stephenson in 1840 and used until October 1965.

Centre
The original Stephenson winding drum at the top of the steep incline on the Crich mineral railway.

Bottom
Whatstandwell Street, Crich, 18 June 1896.

This tramroad was the setting for early trials with William Brunton's famous 'walking locomotive', built at the Butterley Company works in 1813. Brunton himself recorded on 20 November that it 'performs very well'. It was delivered to the Newbottle wagonway near Newcastle where, on 31 July 1815, it burst its boiler, instantly killing two men and a boy and severely scalding and wounding about fifty others, some of whom died.

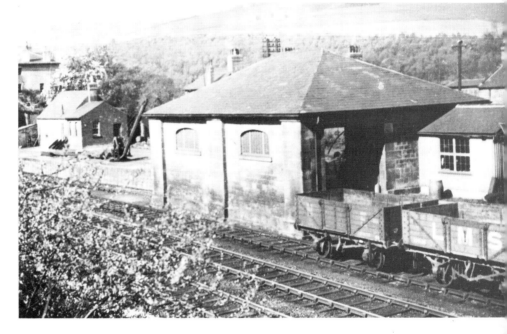

Top
Workmen clearing away charred timberwork after a fire which destroyed the waiting room on No. 3 platform at Ambergate station.

Centre
Ambergate goods yard, looking north, as it was in 1928.

Bottom
Goods yards staff at Ambergate about 1910 with stationmaster Robert Manners fifth from the left, and on his left G. Clutterbuck (foreman), H. Rogers (shunter) and Charles Newbold (the telegraph clerk). Mr Dolman (foreman) is on the extreme left, and third from the left is Frank Roberts (shunter).

Leaving Ambergate via the North Junction and remaining on the original North Midland alignment, the line passes the site of one of the engineering wonders of this portion of the route, for at Bull Bridge village it pierced an embankment carrying the Cromford canal and almost immediately crossed over the River Amber.

In order to achieve this, a single-arch stone aqueduct was constructed, with a towpath for horses, over the line of the railway. To form the aqueduct a large iron trough was floated down the canal to the correct position and then sunk, and by this method disruption of canal traffic was minimised. With the closure of the Cromford canal this aqueduct was subsequently demolished.

In a short distance we reach Crich Junction, from where a line diverges to the right, passing through Butterley, with its historic ironworks and connections with St Pancras, and on to join the main line via the Erewash Valley with junctions at Riddings and Codnor Park respectively, along the north and south sides of a triangle. The northern leg of the triangle is now cut, but the Midland Railway Trust now operates the eastern end of this line and the connection through Codnor Park Junction carries special trains to and from the Midland Railway Centre. All traffic to the Butterley works is now also worked by the Trust.

This link line was built to divert traffic, particularly mineral and goods, from the heavily-used section of main line to Derby and opened on 1 February 1875, passenger operation commencing on the following 1 May. It closed on 2 November 1964 except for Butterley Company operations from Codnor Park Junction to their works on the basis of 'private siding use' only.

Top
Train for Mansfield on the north curve at Ambergate *c*1932 with former Midland 0-4-4T 1347 in charge.

Centre
An engraving of the Bull Bridge aqueduct and bridge.

Bottom
A busy Butterley station *c*1909 with a throng of passengers boarding what is possibly an excursion or special train. The station still hosts steam trains today in its new role as part of the Midland Railway Centre line.

The main line now swings north-wards and on the left can be seen the remains of Wingfield Manor, built by Ralph, Lord Cromwell, about the year 1440 in the reign of Henry VI, and afterwards the seat of the Shrewsburys. It once housed the captive Mary, Queen of Scots, whence she nearly effected a daring escape, with the help of Anthony Babington who was beheaded for his pains.

Wingfield was the next station and, despite being closed since 2 January 1967, the buildings designed by Francis Thompson, and considered by several writers to be the finest of all station houses, still stand though in somewhat parlous state. Built by Radfords of Alfreton in late Georgian style, the station had a well-proportioned central booking hall, with a sculptured clock on the platform side, flanked by bays with low-pitched roofs creating a very attractive overall appeal. The buildings are listed, and will hopefully survive.

The station stands between Oakerthorpe, where once thrived one of three extensive collieries in this locality, and South Wingfield to the north.

The mile-long Shirland branch, which once forked off to the right just north of Wingfield station, led to the colliery of that name which had extensive sidings, providing much traffic for the Midland.

A long embankment now carries the line over two miles across the Amber Valley, with extensive picturesque views on either side, until it reaches Stretton. This station, to the west of the village, was opened by the North Midland as 'Smithy Moor' on 1 June 1841 and was re-named Stretton in a timetable issued on 1 January 1843. It is called 'Shelton' in the Guide to the North Midland Railway issued in 1842, although this must be a misprint!

Top
The ruins of Wingfield Manor, once home of Mary, Queen of Scots, and now open to the public as an ancient monument.

Centre
Francis Thompson's delightful main station building at Wingfield as built in 1839.

Bottom
Caprotti valve-geared 'Stanier' Class 5 4-6-0 44747 heads a Bristol to Newcastle express through Wingfield station, July 1956.

Wingfield Manor

Stretton is a well-built village, six miles south of Chesterfield and in 1851 had one hundred houses with 456 inhabitants which had only increased by 200 people at the turn of the century. Apart from agriculture there was a large ironworks belonging to the Clay Cross Company, of George Stephenson fame, which provided employment up to the early part of this century.

Another railway company had a station at Stretton but this was no real threat to the Midland since it was the two-foot track gauge Ashover Light Railway which opened for business on 6 April 1925. Built to standard gauge structure dimensions, the line was principally used to carry limestone and fluorspar from Ashover and Milltown to the main Clay Cross Company works some 3½ miles away. Passenger traffic was light except at holiday weekends and lasted until 3 October 1931, the last special passenger trains running on 13 September 1936 with a final private tour on 26 August 1947. Stone traffic continued, however, the LMSR being supplied with some 400 tons of ballast per week. When this contract ceased the Ashover quarry closed in January 1950, the line itself closing on 31 March.

The North Midland line reaches its summit just before the entrance to Clay Cross tunnel (1,784 yards), with its Moorish-style castellated stone portals. It cost some £140,000 to build and during its construction coal seams were discovered which caused George Stephenson to form the Clay Cross Company to exploit the rich source of mineral wealth which, before the coming of the railway, could be only slowly transported by road or canal.

It was in Clay Cross tunnel that the absolute block system was first introduced as long ago as the year 1841. During construction in 1839, Stephenson had the electric block telegraph signalling system introduced to him by William Fothergill Cooke,

Top
'Jubilee' class 4-6-0 45576 *Bombay* heads the 12.30pm York to Bristol express through Wingfield, 29 July 1960.

Centre
'Jubilee' 4-6-0 45572 *Eire* approaches Wingfield station with a 'up' express, 11 August 1956.

Bottom
Station approach, Wingfield, showing the stationmaster's house, with a wing for the chief ganger on the left, and the station buildings beyond.

and Wheatstone himself suggested that a candle placed in the window at Glenfield tunnel was hardly sufficient protection for a double-line tunnel such as Clay Cross! Stephenson must have seen the force of the argument and it was arranged that the telegraph should be fitted through the new tunnel to report the arrival and departure of every train. In 1841, Cooke and Wheatstone introduced their electrical instruments with dials plainly showing if the line was clear or blocked, a bell to call signalmen's attention and a red semaphore signal as indication to drivers whether to proceed or stop. From these early beginnings the Midland's network-wide block signalling system was developed.

A group of eighteen houses was built in 1838 by the North Midland Company in East and West Tunnel Rows to house construction workers.

An amusing story has survived from the construction period concerning an excavator who one day entered a public house at Clay Cross with a gallon bottle which he had previously half filled with water and, passing himself off as an overlooker, asked the landlord to add two more quarts of gin to the contents. When this was done he declared to the landlord that he would pay at some future date. Mine host refused the offer and consequently two quarts were removed from the bottle and the wily rascal went on his way with a bottle now containing 'half and half grog'!

In 1837 Stephenson leased plots of land at Clay Cross and set up the firm George Stephenson & Co, of which he remained chairman until his death in 1848, and close links with the North Midland (and subsequently the Midland Railway) Company were formed, the directors recording in

Top
An old 'Bury' 0-4-0 with haystack boiler rests out of use in the siding at Wingfield station. Built in 1846 and used on the LNWR Dunstable branch, it later worked at Wingfield Manor Colliery and is seen here, near the end of its days, on 23 March 1897.

Centre
The wide expanse of the Amber Valley looking north, with the Midland line crossing from left to right in the centre of the picture.

Bottom
Stanier 4-6-0 45260 enters Stretton station from the north with a stopping train, 14 May 1951.

1841 that 'very considerable additions to the traffic may be expected from the Clay Cross Collieries and Coke Works, which are on an extensive scale; the latter moreover will afford the Company the means of obtaining coke at a much lower cost than hitherto . . .'. It should be remembered that in the early years railway locomotives burned coke and not coal.

However, by 1847 the Midland Railway, as successors, were obtaining better coke from Durham and the local product was not in favour, so the Clay Cross Works became involved in smelting local ironstone and extended its activities to ironstone mining.

In 1846 two blast furnaces were erected for the manufacture of iron; a third following in 1854. In later years the Jackson family became sole proprietors and seven coal pits were sunk between 1850 and 1880, whilst the manufacture of iron pipes began in 1864. By the year 1903, some 3,000 tons of coke were being produced each week. Also in the 1850s the Company set up in brickmaking and by 1915 some 5 million bricks were being produced annually. Following the 1947 nationalisation of collieries the company's gas undertaking went the same way the following year, thus removing more than half of its activities.

Today the company continues making spun iron pipes and castings, and has extended its activities to include gravel quarrying with mineral ore washing and separation plants, and also spun concrete pipes.

Stephenson's social conscience was apparent in the style and standard of housing provided for his workers for, as distinct from the two-roomed house in which he was brought up, his Clay Cross houses all had four rooms and for their time were a great advance in hygiene and comfort. In 1856 schools were provided for some fourteen hundred children at a cost of twopence

Top
The main road at Stretton looking towards Chesterfield with 'The White Bear' public house on the left and 'The Three Fishes' on the right. The left fork leads to the station half-a-mile away.

Centre
The Ashover Light Railway station at Ashover with Baldwin 4-6-0 side tank *Joan* in charge of the single coach train, 23 October 1926.

Bottom
Ashover village *c*1910.

per week and the original diminutive Clay Cross hamlet, comprising an isolated turnpike bar and a few isolated houses, grew by 1850 to 600 dwellings housing 3,000 workers, plus a church, three chapels and a Mechanics Institute, the town having been built on top of the tunnel. There was no constable among the entire population, nor apparently was there a need for one!

The railway junction at Clay Cross South was once the hub of a complex series of branches and loop lines serving the large number of collieries and works in the area. Leaving Clay Cross tunnel, a bridge carrying the mile-long branch from Clay Cross Town Goods crossed above the main line to run through the goods sidings and on to Clay Cross main-line station. Services from this depot were withdrawn on 7 October 1963.

Clay Cross South Junction, where the old North Midland line joins the four-track main line along the Erewash Valley, was once a hive of industry. Apart from the Midland's extensive sidings adjacent to both 'up' and 'down' main lines, the Clay Cross Company had its own network of lines joining the Clay Cross Town branch, whilst a little to the north another junction connected both with the Clay Cross Company's No. 4 pit and with the incline which once brought coal down from the Old Williamthorpe colliery.

Between 1869 and 1874 the Midland opened an extensive series of loop lines commencing with the Pilsley branch ,which connected that colliery with the main Erewash Valley line just north of Doe Hill. This branch extended to link in with other collieries, notably Heath and Holmwood & Hardwick. Then, by means of the Pilsley extension part way along, connected with a triangular junction to link in with the previously mentioned Willamthorpe colliery and, by means of a northern loop on to the main line north of Clay Cross station, also linked up with Grassmoor, Bonds Main and Calow collieries.

Top
The castellated north portal of Clay Cross tunnel.

Centre
'Miles of trucks' at Clay Cross – Nos. 2 and 3 Collieries *c*1907.

Bottom
Clay Cross Company official postcard illustrating the man-handling of coal tubs in the early part of this century.

High Street, Clay Cross

The station at Clay Cross (142 miles 19 chains) originally had a staggered platform layout, with the 'up' platform slightly to the south of the 'down' where the main simple rectangular-style station building was located, immediately opposite to the water storage tank and pumphouse, also built in matching style. This station, under the watchful eye of stationmaster Robert Jeffrey, had a service in the 1850s of two 'up' and three 'down' passenger trains daily, with two each way on Sundays, enabling passengers to reach Derby in the south and Leeds to the north.

The station remained in this form until May 1879 when the new buildings and platform layout came into use, consisting of one island platform and adjacent side platforms. The builder was John Garlick and the cost £3,119 4s 2d.

By 1940 a service of some thirteen local trains daily each way was provided, increasing to seventeen by 1962, serving Derby, Nottingham and Chesterfield, with some through services. The station closed for goods traffic on 4 May 1964 and for passengers on 2 January 1967.

Continuing northwards from Clay Cross the railway passes through an area of mines and industrial premises, including the large Avenue Works and sidings on the 'down' side, coming eventually to Hasland where a goods station was situated until its closure on 3 May 1965, and just beyond the junction for the branch linking in the local colliery loop lines, with its connections to the nearby Great Central Railway.

Half-a-mile north of the junction formerly stood the compact locomotive depot of Hasland, location of a stud of

Top
High Street, Clay Cross is depicted in this postcard view taken just before the First World War. Singer sewing machines are on offer in the shop on the left and Co-op Pelaw bun flour in the grocers' on the right.

Centre
Clay Cross South Junction, with the line from Derby swinging in from the right to join the line from the Erewash Valley on the left. Class 4F 0-6-0 43986 on a 'down' freight passes 'Austerity' 2-8-0 90722 on an up freight in this scene photographed on 6 October 1962.

Bottom
The original Thompson designed North Midland station at Clay Cross with the pump house on the left. A new station replaced this one in 1879.

locomotives utilised to work local services. The earliest record of a Chesterfield depot is a minute dated 15 October 1861 ordering that plans be prepared for an engine house and turntable to cover the working of passenger traffic generated by the opening of the Erewash Valley main line. The name Hasland first appears in connection with a roundhouse, together with a row of cottages for the men, which was opened in 1875. In 1880 Hasland's stud of locomotives comprised thirty-four 0-6-0 goods engines and four 2-4-0s and by 1896 this had increased to forty-three 0-6-0s with ten 2-4-0 passenger tender and seven 0-6-0 tank engines. By the end of 1920 there were nineteen 2-4-0s, thirty-five 0-6-0 tender and six tank engines, and a single 0-4-0 tank, these latter two types being used, among other duties, to shunt local ironworks. In the 1950s sixteen of the Garratt 2-6-6-2 articulated locomotives were allocated (mainly from Toton) to work heavy iron-ore traffic between Wellingborough and York and also turns to Gowhole, but these had been withdrawn by 1958. The depot closed on 7 September 1964 and the site is now a local authority refuse tip – from a passing train it is well-nigh impossible to realise it was formerly a thriving locomotive depot.

Hasland village is somewhat scattered, and in 1851 some 1,200 inhabitants occupied 280 houses. By the turn of the century the population had increased considerably to over 7,000 due to the change from a rural village to an industrial centre.

On either side of the line lie other important places of interest and just to the south-west of Hasland lies Wingerworth which, whilst not meriting a station of its own because of its proximity to Chesterfield, has its own Hall, seat of the Brailsford, Curzon and Hunloke families and later still, the Wilmers. One member

Top
Clay Cross station, looking north *c*1906.

Centre
Clay Cross station, looking north as Stanier 2-8-0 48395 approaches with an 'up' mineral train during the ASLE&F strike, 2 June 1955.

Bottom
Another Clay Cross Company postcard depicting collier Territorial Army volunteers at Clay Cross station waiting to board the train which took them to a fortnight's camp in the Peak of Derbyshire. Clay Cross No. 4 pit is in the background.

No. 110.]   [See Nos. 109 & 114.
COLLIER-TERRITORIALS.
Getters of the renowned "C.X.C. Gold Medal" Coal entraining at Clay Cross Station for the Peak of Derbyshire for a fortnight's camp. No. 4 Pit in the background.

of the Hunloke family had the doubtful distinction of falling dead at the feet of James I in Ilkeston whilst attending a royal reception. It is an ancient stone mansion rebuilt by the third Baronet Hunloke between 1726 and 1729, whilst nearby is the ancient church dedicated to All Saints. The parish contains several small hamlets and in 1851 boasted 95 houses with 463 inhabitants which remained little changed in numbers up to the turn of the century.

Also in the parish were iron mines, a foundry and the large collieries of the Wingerworth Coal and the Clay Cross Companies, both of which provided much traffic for the Midland.

Across the wide Scarsdale Valley stands Bolsover Castle, with its Norman tower and Elizabethan replica of the original castle built in the eleventh century by William Peveril, ancestor of Sir Walter Scott's *Peveril of the Peak*, and upon whose foundation it rests. Later, having passed into the hands of the Crown, the original castle was given as a wedding present by Richard the Lionheart to John his brother.

A mere four miles or so away stands Hardwick Hall whose appearance initiated the old rhyme 'Hardwick Hall, more glass than wall' because of its countless windows which sparkle and shine in a myriad of hues when reflecting the sun's rays. Now nearly 400 years old, it was erected by the famous 'Bess of Hardwick', otherwise Elizabeth, Countess of Shrewsbury, who had four husbands and was the ancestor of the Dukedoms of Devonshire, Newcastle, Portland, Kingston and Norfolk. She was a shrewd businesswoman of whom Elizabeth I said 'there is no lady in this

Top
Double-framed Kirtley 0-6-0 541, superbly decorated with flags, foliage and a crown by the Hasland and Staveley Locomotive Depot's staff, possibly in celebration of the Coronation of King Edward VII on 9 August 1902.

Centre
Avenue sidings, north of Clay Cross, 15 June 1957, as the 'up' Edinburgh express, headed by Midland 2P 4-4-0, 40436 piloting Class 5 4-6-0 45447, passes 'Stanier' Class 8F 2-8-0 48358 on an 'up' freight.

Bottom
Meet of the hounds at Wingerworth Hall (although no hounds are in evidence in this *c*1912 picture). The boy on the pony is clearly starting young!

land that I better love and like'. Her magnificent tomb, erected to her instructions before her death and which she frequently visited, stands in Derby Cathedral.

In a short distance the line reaches Chesterfield which derives its name from Castle Hill at Tapton, just north of the town to which 'castle' – or 'chester' in Roman terms – it was the 'field'. Its most famous and obvious claim to fame is the twisted spire of the Church of All Saints, 228 feet high, eight-sided, and built of timber covered with lead plates set in zig-zag fashion. The spire now has an obvious twist and is nearly eight feet out of perpendicular due to the sun's heat warping the wood, which is inadequately braced. The distortion can be seen clearly from the south as the Midland approaches the town.

Next the Midland passed under the viaduct which once carried the misleadingly-named Lancashire, Derbyshire and East Coast Railway Company tracks over both it and the adjacent Great Central Company's line by means of brick arches, lattice girders and a huge bowstring span, and then continued into their station at Chesterfield Market Place, which opened on 8 March 1897. Driving force behind this scheme was William Arkwright who wished to develop coal reserves on his estate to the east of the town, and other coal owners soon joined in. The plan was to link Chesterfield with Warrington in the west and, via Lincoln, the new docks in the east to be built at Sutton-on-Sea. In the event, neither the Lincolnshire end nor the route to the west was built. The LDEC line passed into Great Central ownership in 1907, and, with further added connections, remained open for passenger use until 3 December 1951 and for goods traffic until 4 March 1957. A small part of the network remains for goods and mineral traffic today but the Chesterfield station was demolished in April 1973.

Top
Bolsover Castle, near Chesterfield, is featured in this photograph *c*1919.

Centre
Slip coaches for Chesterfield being detached from a 'down' express near Horns Bridge *c*1911.

Bottom
Veteran Kirtley 0-6-0 2300, built in August 1850 and still at work, heading an 'up' coal train southwards from Chesterfield in 1911.

The Midland then proceeds over the remains of the former Great Central line from Heath through Grassmoor to Chesterfield, part of a 4¾-mile section opened on 3 July 1893, which converted the GCR Chesterfield line into a complete loop off their main line. Grassmoor station opened on 1 November of that year.

Continuing, the Midland reaches the former junction converging from the left which brought the branch from Brampton Goods depot (147 miles 13 chains) to join with the main line. This served a number of varied companies including the Midland's own gas works and was vested in the Midland in 1871. An incline connected Boythorpe Colliery to the branch.

The North Midland station at Chesterfield opened with the line on 11 May 1840 and was originally a most attractive building in Jacobean style, standing on the west side of the tracks. Designed by Francis Thompson, it was built by Leather & Waring. The large projecting centre bay had a gable end on the single platform with a pair of smaller flanking bays set back on each side. At the south end of the platform stood an attractive block of buildings housing the main water storage tank with workshops and a steam pumphouse.

In connection with the new direct route to Sheffield, opened on 1 February 1870, the Midland decided to build a completely new station about 100 yards further north (146 miles 20 chains from St Pancras). Work began in 1869 and the new station was opened on 3 May 1870, the earlier building being closed and subsequently demolished. The new

Top
Chesterfield's three railways meet at Horns Bridge. The railway in the foreground is the Great Central line from Chesterfield Central, the Midland main line crosses the middle of the picture with the rear of a northbound freight train visible, whilst on the high viaduct of the LD&ECR a passenger train, which has just left Chesterfield Market Place station, heads towards Shirebrook. The Horns Hotel, which probably gave the spot its name, is on the extreme right.

Centre
Francis Thompson's delightful original station at Chesterfield, which was replaced by a new one opened on 2 May 1870.

Bottom
Derby 2-2-2 728 at the original Chesterfield station between September 1867 and September 1868. Note the addition of a large awning to the station and alterations to the stonework to accommodate it.

station had platforms either side of the twin-track main line, passenger access to the 'up' platform being by means of a subway, and a bay at the north end of the 'down' platform and the south end of the 'up' platform. Its builder was Archibald Neill and the work was not completed until 1872, at a cost of £11,803. The present goods lines pass behind the main 'up' platform to the east. The station was modernised during 1964–5, many of the earlier facilities disappearing. Passenger services from Chesterfield have always been good, with direct connections to the south and west as well as to all points north. Even in North Midland days there were seven trains daily to the north via Leeds and York, and to the south via Derby. The opening of the Erewash Valley line throughout on 1 May 1862 also gave a more direct route to Nottingham, and to London via Trent and Leicester.

By 1910 there were five through trains to London, and through services to Bristol with connections to the west of England, and it boasted a through service beyond Edinburgh to Aberdeen. Today the station hosts the Inter-City High Speed trains with good services north, south and west, although passengers from Manchester must go forward via Sheffield since a regular direct service along the Hope Valley is no more, the only exceptions being the Harwich boat train and a service to Barrow.

Chesterfield is an old market town with Roman origins and was once an important trading centre for iron and lead, but it was the arrival of the North Midland Railway and George Stephenson which set the seal on its progress. He decided in 1840 that he would live near to the town at Tapton House where he died of pleurisy on 12 August 1848 aged 67. He is buried under the altar in Holy Trinity church.

Top
'Jubilee' 4-6-0 45616 *Malta GC* of Kentish Town shed heads an 'up' express through Chesterfield, 3 September 1955.

Centre
Articulated Beyer Garratt 2-6-6-2 47988 with rotary coal bunker enters Chesterfield station with an 'up' mineral train c1956. These powerful locomotives were built to haul heavy coal and mineral trains from Toton and surrounding colliery districts to London.

Bottom
The interior of Chesterfield Midland station in all its interesting detail is shown on this postcard written and sent 12 October 1912.

Chesterfield had a population of some 7,100 in 1851 which had risen steeply to 27,185 by the turn of the century and which today exceeds 70,000. Many of its older buildings survive, some clad in mock Tudor timber, and it has a classical town hall built as late as 1938. The Stephenson Memorial Hall, opened in his memory in 1879, now houses the Civic Theatre and Public Library. It has several parks of which Queen's Park has a fine sports stadium and many other recreational activities including cricket and football, Chesterfield being at present in the Third Division of the Football League.

Notable among local industries is Markham & Company whose works lie to the East of the line. It is an old established firm, founded as Oliver & Co. Ltd., mill and colliery engineers, which today carries out a large variety of heavy engineering work.

Top
Chesterfield looking across what were then fields towards the west, as it appeared in September 1899. The station occupies the centre of this fascinating official Midland photograph.

Centre
A view of West Bars, Chesterfield, looking towards the market hall in the early part of this century.

Bottom
24,000hp double runner turbines at the Chesterfield works of Markham & Co Ltd.

3
Through the
Hope Valley

The competitor in Chesterfield was the Great Central whose station was opened on 4 June 1892 (although the loop to Heath was not completed until 23 July 1893), but services on this line were definitely inferior to those on the Midland. Known merely as 'Chesterfield' until the amalgamation of 1907, it became Chesterfield Central on 1 January of that year, and at the same time the LD&ECR station had the words 'Market Place' added to its title upon its becoming part of the Great Central empire.

Leaving Chesterfield station, with the remains of the Great Central line now hardly traceable on the left, the line reaches Tapton Junction (146 miles 69 chains) where the old North Midland line to Leeds diverges on the right from the later, direct line to Sheffield, construction of which began in response to pressure from the Mayor and Corporation of that city. The new line was officially opened on Tuesday, 1 February 1870, at a cost of around £1.2 million. The Act for building the line suffered the usual delays, mainly due to opposition from various landowners and other vested interests, but was finally given Royal Assent on 25 July 1864 and contracts were awarded for its construction. Eckersley & Bayliss of Chapel-en-le-Frith were contracted to build the section from Chesterfield to the south end of Bradway tunnel for £91,700, whilst the contract for the tunnel, together with the section beyond as far as Beauchief (Contracts Nos. 3 and 4), went to George Thomson of Cheltenham. The first sod above Bradway tunnel was turned exactly a year after the Act was granted, and

Previous page
Directors' tour of the Dore and Chinley line at the east end of Totley tunnel, 10 August 1893. The train is composed of three wagons belonging to the contractor Thomas Oliver. These have been specially fitted with seats, and are hauled by 'Hunslet' 0-6-0 saddle tank engine *Nene*, built in 1881, one of the contractors' locomotives used during the line's construction.

Top
The Great Central railway station in Chesterfield – note the period advertisements and 'decorated' horse-drawn parcels van on the left.

Centre
LMS 2-6-0 42903 heading a freight train into Chesterfield Midland, September 1955.

Bottom
Stanier 2-8-0 48281 of Normanton shed on a 'down' freight train passing through Chesterfield Midland station, 24 April 1961. Note twisted spire on right.

Top
'Jubilee' 4-6-0 45651 *Shovell* of Bristol shed approaching Chesterfield with the 4.45pm Bradford to Bristol express, 13 June 1957.

Centre
45651 *Shovell* features again in this view of Sheepbridge station with the 4.08pm Sheffield to Derby stopping train. Note 148 milepost on right.

Bottom
A smartly-turned-out 0-6-0 well tank locomotive 2064, built in 1860 by Manning Wardle for the Sheepbridge Iron Company. This locomotive was purchased by the Midland in October 1870 and was in service until 1900.

work continued apace. Shanty towns sprang up along the route with huts for navvies, blacksmiths' and joiners' shops, like the small settlement at Bradway Bar, complete with 'tommy shops' where workers were compelled to purchase their goods because they were paid by ticket rather than in real money. The usual friction between navvies and the local populace resulted in quite a few disturbances, particularly in the Dronfield area on Saturday nights when, on one occasion, a pitched battle was fought with local miners; sharpened broom handles and handkerchiefs weighted with stones being considered fair weapons!

On this new route the first station out of Chesterfield was Sheepbridge (147 miles 77 chains), opened on 1 August 1870 a little after the rest of the line, since no station had originally been planned for this location.

Built by Chadwick & Thirlwell, Sheepbridge had five services daily to Chesterfield and the south, and six to Sheffield of which four went through to Leeds. One morning and one afternoon train was provided in each direction on Sundays. On 8 October 1897 the station was renamed Sheepbridge and Whittington Moor, reverting to its original title on 18 June 1951. It was closed to passenger traffic on 2 January 1967.

From the old North Midland line and by means of a triangular junction, a branch parallel to the new line, but more to the east, ran to Sheepbridge Goods and from thence to serve the Sheepbridge Coal and Iron Company's sidings before continuing in a north-westerly direction and splitting to serve the former Monkwood and Nesfield collieries.

Passing over this branch, acquired by the Midland in 1870, the line ran through the 92-yard long Broomhouse tunnel (opened out in 1969) and, passing the Unstone branch sidings

serving a local colliery and mills in a
loop line which rejoined the main line
that south of Dronfield, the railway
then passes over Unstone Viaduct
(No. 14) and reaches Unstone station
(150 miles 14 chains). The contract for
the construction of Unston station (as
it was known until 1 July 1908, when it
became Unstone), along with those at
Dronfield, Abbey Houses (later
Beauchief), Ecclesall and Heeley went
to J. & E. Wood. All were opened
with the line.

Unstone became an unstaffed halt
from 4 February 1946, closed for
passengers on 29 October 1951 and
completely from 1 September 1961.
Little survives of the station today
save the remnants of the 'up' platform
upon which industrial premises now
stand.

Unstone village grew considerably
as a direct result of the arrival of the
railway and the associated growth of
local industry, particularly the
coalfields. From less than 900 in 1861,
the population rose to over 2,300 by
1881, with a decline to around 1800 by
the year 1900. This century has again
seen a gradual increase.

The railway now climbs steeply up a
1 in 90 bank to the next station,
Dronfield (151 miles 44 chains) which
has recently had a new lease of life,
being re-opened on 5 January 1981
under a local transport development
scheme supported by the North East
Derbyshire District and Derbyshire
County Councils. Councillors G. W.
Haslam and G. N. Wilson, Chairmen
of the respective councils, performed
the opening ceremony.

The old buildings have been swept
away and accommodation comprises a
single stone-built bus-type shelter with
seats on each platform, whilst the 'up'
and 'down' sides are linked by an iron
girder footbridge resting on blue
bricks and reached by means of
wooden stairways.

Situated at the north end of an
embankment which skirts the east side
of the village, and just beyond the
bridge which carries the line over the
main road, the station had been closed
to passenger traffic from 2 January
1967 and for goods since 1 May the
same year until this new initiative
commenced, involving supportive

Top
Unstone viaduct which carries the Midland
main line over the river Drone as it
approaches Unstone station – view looking
south-east.

Centre
The overbridge south of Unstone station
with a fine Midland slotted post type signal.

Bottom
An enlargement of the centre portion of
the previous photograph showing Unstone
station about 1887.

Top
The remains of Unstone station 'up' platform, now occupied by the workshops of a local engineering firm.

Centre
Unstone village, looking south. The Midland line and site of the former station is to the right.

Bottom
Dronfield station as it was in Midland days, looking north. Access to the station is now via a small modern booking office on the 'up' platform.

grant-aid. It has a service at peak times of seven trains daily to Sheffield with six to Chesterfield, and two and one respectively on Saturdays. In 1985 fares to either Sheffield or Chesterfield were 45p for adults and 23p for children but one could purchase a multi-journey ticket available for twenty single trips in either direction for £8.10p.

Dronfield is an ancient market town lying on the River Drone which, in the nineteenth century, became almost swamped by the growing coal and iron industries. The early Gothic church is dedicated to St John the Baptist and, with its fourteenth-century features, may be the successor of an earlier one at Unstone. It has a fine 138-ft high spire, a clerestory roof to beautiful nave arcades, a unique pair of fourteenth-century memorial brasses to brothers Thomas and Richard Gomfrey, and a fine oak screen by Tideswell craftsman, Advent Hunstone. The town has several houses from the sixteenth and seventeenth centuries, a grammar school dating back to 1579, and during this century has become fringed with modern housing estates with a new Recreation Centre opened in July 1973 as part of the new town centre development plan. In 1851 it had a population of 2,469 which had risen by 1900 to 3,809 and today stands at over 26,000. Local engineering industries include Edward Lucas & Son Ltd, established in 1790 as makers of malleable castings.

After crossing the main road by means of a bridge made of cast-iron arched beams, about a mile north of Dronfield the line enters Bradway tunnel (1 mile 267 yards) cut through millstone grit. Whilst excavating this tunnel it was established that 16,000 gallons of water flowed every hour from the springs uncovered during the operation and seven pumping engines, working day and night, were required to keep the workings clear. The problem was not solved until small heading tunnels were completed to carry the water away. Half of the tunnel had been completed by 3 June 1867 but shortly afterwards the contractor, George Thomson, died so

his brother and partner Peter came from Liverpool to complete the work.

Leaving the tunnel the line reaches a triangular junction where the main route to Sheffield curves away to the right. This marks the limit of our interest in the main line to the north, for swinging away sharply to the west at Dore South Junction the route to Manchester takes us via the abrupt south curve of the triangle on to the Midland's Dore and Chinley line which leads into the heart of the Peak. This line was opened throughout on 6 November 1893 for goods traffic and on 13 May 1894 the first through express trains were run between Sheffield and Manchester, local traffic commencing on 1 June 1894, the Midland having taken over complete ownership of the line on 2 April 1894. The railway was built to provide a much better link between these two main centres of population, since until its opening most travellers had used the Manchester, Sheffield & Lincolnshire Railway's line over the Woodhead route, with its best journey time of well under two hours.

Originally promoted in 1872 from Dore to Hassop, a mile north of Bakewell, the revised second scheme for the 20 miles 8 chains line to Chinley was introduced before Parliament in 1884, promoted by the independent Dore and Chinley Railway Company, and would have failed for lack of sufficient financial support but for Midland interest. In 1888 the scheme was vested in the Midland and work on the line began immediately. Construction work included two of the longest tunnels on the Midland system, namely Totley tunnel (3 miles 950 yards) and Cowburn tunnel (2 miles 182 yards). There was also a need for severe gradients, including long stretches of 1 in 100.

Passing via the south curve through the short Dore tunnel (91 yards) the line joins the west curve from the Sheffield direction at Dore West Junction (154 miles 64 chains) and in a little over a mile enters the east end of the tunnel which passes beneath Totley Moor to emerge at Grindleford

Top
'Jubilee' Class 4-6-0 45616 *Malta GC* approaches Dronfield with the 10.05am Edinburgh to St Pancras express, 12 May 1956.

Centre
Dronfield station in LMS days, looking south.

Bottom
Dronfield village, looking east, with the church of St John the Baptist centre right. Modern housing has now covered many of the surrounding fields seen here.

station situated hard against the tunnel mouth.

Drilling of the tunnel began on 24 September 1888 and water was struck after only eight feet. Four permanent and three temporary shafts were sunk within three-quarters-of-a-mile of the eastern end and the largest permanent shaft resulted in 26,000 gallons of water being pumped out each hour to keep it clear. During the worst period of construction, over 5 million gallons of water were being pumped away daily. 163 tons of gelignite were used during the construction and lining of the bore, which was carried out in each direction from 51 water free sites, eastern and western headings meeting on 19 October 1892. It was completed on 4 August 1893, and track work throughout was completed the following 2 September.

During construction work on this section of line, particularly in the area around Totley tunnel, outbreaks of scarlet fever, diptheria and small-pox occurred, which put the construction camps under quarantine for a time. Because of the drainage difficulties in the tunnel a typhoid epidemic also took its toll. One navvy, 'Bumble-Bee Dick' by nickname, died of both heart failure and pneumonia while at work on the tunnel in 1893.

Totley tunnel is of such exceptional length that when it was opened a specially devised electrical communication system was installed in addition to the block system, to enable drivers, firemen, guards, and even platelayers working in the tunnel, to communicate with the signalmen at each end of the tunnel in the event of an incident. A special wire had merely to be cut to activate alarm bells in both signal boxes and cause traffic to be halted. The same system was also applied to the shorter tunnel at Cowburn, further along the line.

The Midland said of the new line: 'It has opened up quite a new portion of the ever-attractive Peak district which, from a picturesque point of view is in many points equal to, if not superior to the old part. The ground, so far as the general tourist is

Top
Dore and Totley station in 1939, looking north as 'Jubilee' 4-6-0 5628 *Somaliland* heads an 'up' express towards the South Junction.

Centre
Dore and Totley station *c*1889, before it was rebuilt to provide the link via the west curve with the Dore and Chinley line from the Sheffield direction.

Bottom
48466, a Stanier Class 8F 2-8-0, emerging from Dore tunnel No. 1 and passing Dore & Totley South Junction signal box with an 'up' express freight train, 19 June 1954.

concerned, may be considered quite virgin, no doubt because the means of access, until the opening of the new railway, has been anything but inviting. But to the ardent pilgrim who is not averse to rock and hill climbing, not deterred by slippery ways and the freaks of wind and weather, an ample reward in the delights of bracing air, the sight of woodland and valley scenery and extensive landscapes is to be found worthy of the toil taken . . .'

Totley village, adjacent to the east end of the tunnel, was originally a scattered township with some industry in the form of lead smelting, a chemical works belonging to T. Tinker & Company and in earlier times a fire-brick manufactory. In 1851 a mere 403 persons living in 83 houses inhabited the locality and the number of people had swelled to 912 by the year 1900. It is now largely a dormitory area for Sheffield.

Where the line emerges from the west end of Totley Tunnel stands the attractive station of Grindleford (158 miles 69 chains). Opened with the line it stands at the entrance to the Hope Valley which has always held a special appeal for tourists, hikers and cyclists anxious to get away from the smoke and grime of the large towns on the fringe of the Peak District. It is mainly for this reason that this station, like the others between here and Chinley,

Top
Another view of the Directors' tour of the new line on 10 August 1893, this time between Totley Tunnel East and Dore & Totley West Junction.

Bottom
Construction work in progress at Grindleford station and the west end of Totley tunnel (then called 'Padley Tunnel'), 29 August 1893. The bridge carrying the main road over the line has already been completed.

has survived, although sadly it was the choice of this line which sealed the eventual fate of the other Midland one through Bakewell and Miller's Dale, which will be covered later in our story.

All the stations on the Dore and Chinley line were built by Walker & Slater, building contractors, at a total cost of £11,500.

The village of Grindleford itself is more than a mile to the south of the station and, in fact, the nearest village is Nether Padley with the restored Padley Chapel, once the private sanctuary of Padley Manor and a little beyond it, across Eyam Moor, the celebrated village of that name.

Eyam suffered in the grip of the Great Plague from September 1665 to October 1666 during which time 259 from a population of 350 were struck down. By self-imposed isolation and led by their rector, the Reverend William Mompesson, the villagers ensured the plague did not spread, and a simple memorial service is held in nearby Cucklett Dell, where the villagers worshipped at the time, on the last Sunday in August each year to commemorate their great sacrifice.

The charming village, with its stocks, its hall, its fine church and superb Saxon cross in the churchyard, is a haunt of visitors, particularly during its well-dressings held on the Saturday before the Plague Commemoration Service.

Grindleford, once a quiet remote village, has in this century become very much a dormitory for Sheffield with at first businessmen seeking a country refuge, whilst in this present age it is used by both professional person and tradesman alike, although travel is now more by motor-car than by the formerly much-used Midland suburban services which at one time were both convenient and regular. The village is centred upon the bridge, an eighteenth-century replacement of an early fifteenth-century construction, which afforded a crossing place over the Derwent on the road between

GRINDLEFORD STATION.

Top
Grindleford station just before the First World War. The message on this postcard, sent to New Cumnock, Ayrshire, reads: 'We shall be home on Wednesday evening. Please have some supper ready about 7.15pm.'

Centre
LMS Compound 4-4-0 1144 emerges from Totley tunnel into Grindleford station with a 'down' local train in 1948.

Bottom
The plague cottages at Eyam village with the church beyond. The plague is thought to have arrived from London in a box of old clothes.

Sheffield and Eyam. To the north lies Longshaw Lodge, built as a hunting box for the Duke of Rutland, and around it the National Trust property of Longshaw Moors, with its famous sheepdog trials, held on the first Thursday in September, which attract both local and national entrants.

The line sweeps to the north, closely following the river, and in less than two miles runs into Hathersage station, set in majestic surroundings with the sharp summit of Stanage Edge rising on the right, close to the boundary between Derbyshire and Yorkshire.

Set some 160 miles 60 chains from St Pancras by the direct route and at an altitude of 540 feet above sea level, Hathersage station was a simple affair with wooden board platforms and with identical timber-faced buildings on stone bases with part stone end walls and chimney stack, which stood on both 'up' and 'down' platforms, like those at Bamford and Edale. The service in 1903 comprised ten 'down' and ten 'up' trains, of which five were between Sheffield and Manchester while three ran direct to Buxton via Peak Forest giving various connections at Chinley. From Hathersage Sheffield could be reached in 24 minutes; Manchester in 65 minutes; Liverpool in a further 50 minutes; and Buxton was just 48 minutes away.

Today's local traveller to intermediate stations has a choice of nine trains, although all are now Second Class only 'all stations stoppers' with a Sunday service of four trains each way. The Hathersage area is famous for its gorgeous scenery, the village nestling along the hillside to the north of the railway, and commanding it is the fourteenth-century church of St Michael with brasses to the Eyre family, of which Robert of Highlow Hall is said to have built a house for each of his seven sons, all within sight of the Hall. The glass in the church vestry windows by Kempe was brought here from Derwent chapel when it was flooded to make the Ladybower Reservoir. In the churchyard, between two yews, is

Top
Hathersage station stands ready to receive an 'up' train in the early part of this century – a view looking east.

Centre
The goods siding is derelict and the station has lost some of its Midland features such as gas lamps, posters and fencing in this view of Hathersage, looking west, 31 May 1971.

Bottom
'Up' banana special at Hathersage hauled by Midland 0-6-0 3797 in the summer of 1911.

the grave of Little John, a native of the village and Robin Hood's faithful lieutenant. When opened in 1780 it was found to contain bones of a very large size including a thigh bone 32 inches long. The cottage from where he is reported to have shot his last arrow stands nearby and his bow and cap were said to have hung in the church for many years.

Local industry included the manufacture of needles from locally drawn wire and paper and the village had a population of nearly 1,800 in 1831 which declined by the turn of the century, with the fall back in local industry, to 1,135 and today stands at some 1,450.

Nearby stands Moorseats House, the Moor House of Charlotte Bronte's *Jane Eyre*, for Charlotte stayed in Hathersage with her friend Ellen Nussey, whose brother was the vicar. North Lees Hall nearby is probably 'Thornfield Hall' in the same work.

The road through the village was once thronged with horse-drawn carts and wagons ferrying goods and supplies into the Hope valley from Sheffield, but with the opening of the railway this trade almost ceased and the old carrier carts and omnibuses were laid aside. Local inhabitants rejoiced briefly when the price of heavier goods and coal fell, and they could themselves more easily travel to the city, but within a quarter of a century road transport became motorised and capable of quicker journey times and was beginning to assert itself again.

In the early part of 1882 the road between Fox House and Hathersage became almost impassable for carriages due to the antics of a large steam traction-engine towing two huge trucks laden with goods from Dronfield to places along the valley. A public outcry ensued after a boy was killed, a mail-cart overturned and one of two other young persons in a private carriage died after it collided with 'the hideous abomination', as a chronicler

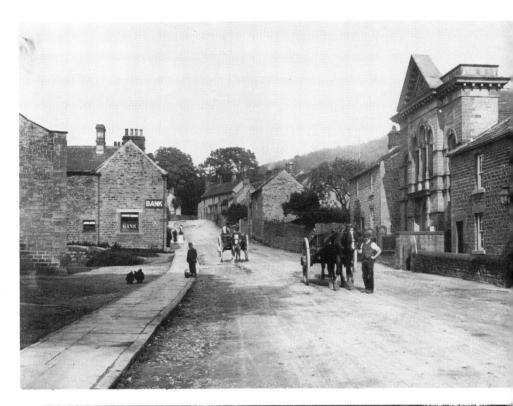

Top
The Midland's own photographer caught this delightful Hathersage street scene on 22 July 1895 – a time when village life was untroubled by the motor car, when hens could scratch in the roadside verge and the only horsepower on the roads was on four legs.

Centre
The reputed grave of Robin Hood's chief lieutenant, Little John, in Hathersage churchyard.

Bottom
The peace of Hathersage station is disturbed as 'Compound' 4-4-0 41170 enters at the head of the 2.28pm Chinley to Sheffield stopping train, 25 April 1955.

of the time so described it and added, 'It is inconceivable that such a monstrous deformity should be allowed to grind and snort its way, as a regular institution through scenes into which the introduction of railways has been loudly decried on aesthetic grounds.' The comment says much of Victorian sensibilities and one wonders how the same chronicler reacted when the Midland invaded this precious valley!

The bulk of today's traffic is again on the roads and the family motorist uses his convenient car rather than the train to see the beauties of the valley, although hikers, in good numbers, still frequent the rail services. For hill walkers and hikers almost any form of dress is of course considered 'acceptable', and this old poem of the 1880's may raise a smile:

A holiday is a dismal sham if your
*   clothes are fit to be seen,*
For how can anyone let themselves go
*   if they have to keep themselves clean.*
Come out unspeakable old tweed suit,
*   beloved and ancient skirt.*
That which is shrunk need fear no rain,
*   that which is torn no hurt.*
Come out with me to the hills and the sea
*   and collect a little more dirt!*

Since those days members of various rambling clubs from nearby towns, as well as individual family groups, have arrived in the area by train, omnibus, charabanc, car or cycle and taken to these hills to spend the day either by following the quiet winding lanes or cutting across country, scrambling over rocks, mounds and streams, to enjoy the great variety of enchanting natural beauty which opens up to the view on every side.

From Hathersage the line crosses Hathersage viaduct and runs in an almost straight line to the next station, Bamford (162 miles 42 chains). This village lies beneath the long gritstone outcrop of Bamford Edge and has fine views of Win Hill, which rises to 1,520 feet and overlooks five dales. It has solid gritstone houses with well-kept gardens, and local industry was once

Top
Picnic in the Peak – a family group from Derby enjoy a meal in beautiful surroundings at an unknown location *c*1904.

Centre
Bamford station, looking towards Chinley, 31 May 1971. The booking office is situated on the road overbridge alongside the 'down' line.

Bottom
Bamford station as seen from the road overbridge in September 1919, looking towards Dore as a double-headed goods train passes through the station.

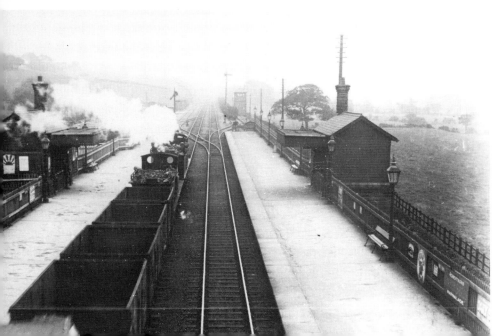

centred on cotton mills. Nearby, on Low Peak plateau, leadmining was formerly carried out. A population of 500 was in residence by the year 1900.

Bamford lies at the foot of a long valley which brings the River Derwent, rising near Bleaklow, down from the moors on the Derbyshire-Yorkshire border into the Hope valley. In its course a series of large dams has been constructed during the present century by the Derwent Valley Water Board to supply water to the two counties, of which the Ladybower Reservoir, officially opened in 1945 by King George VI, was the last. It is most famous perhaps as the site of practice runs by the RAF using Barnes Wallis' 'bouncing bomb', successfully used in the destruction of the Mohne and Eder dams in Germany during the last war. Beneath its waters now lie the villages of Derwent Chapel and Ashopton, the remains of which can still be exposed in times of drought.

Before the dam came the traveller could stay at the Lady Bower Inn, a clean and comfortable hostelry, set in the midst of unrivalled natural beauty, and for half-a-crown (12½p) a day's good fishing could be had in the Lady Bower Brook or the River Ashop.

During the construction of the Howden (opened 1912) and Derwent (opened 1916) reservoirs further up the valley some 1¼ million tons of stone quarried at Grindleford were moved by tramway to that station and thence via the Midland line to a location between Bamford and Hope where an interchange point was established. This remained until 1916 when construction work was completed and was later re-established during work on the Ladybower Reservoir.

Bamford station lost its goods facilities on 31 January 1966 and became an unstaffed halt from 7 September 1969.

Leaving Bamford the line crosses the Derwent just once, by means of an iron girder bridge, and approaches Hope station (for Castleton and Bradwell). A mile beyond Hope station a 'mineral only' line swings in from the left, which carries cement from the extensive Earles Cement

Top
A peaceful street scene in Bamford village as seen by the Midland's official photographer on 23 July 1895, whilst on a tour of the Dore and Chinley line for advertising material.

Centre
BR 'Standard' 4-6-0 73043 stands at Bamford station with a south bound stopping train, 17 March 1962.

Bottom
Hope station, looking towards Chinley in the early part of this century.

factory two miles away, established in 1928, which can be seen clearly in the distance from this point on the line.

Hope village lies in the valley to which it gives its name and near the point where the River Noe meets Peakshole Water. Only a mile away is Brough, once called 'Navio' as a remote outpost of the Roman empire. There are many Roman remains from 'Navio' in Buxton Museum. A settlement in Saxon times and with a church dedicated to St Peter containing some fine glass, Hope was once a thriving market town with a number of fairs, including a Great Fair for cattle, cloth, ironmongery and pedlary which was formerly held on 13 May each year, with a statute for the hiring of farm labourers and servants on an annual basis.

It was a large village even before the coming of the Midland, for the population of the parish in 1841 was 4,434 persons, of whom 430 lived in the township which had fallen to 382 by the turn of the century as people moved out to seek better paid jobs in the industrial regions.

The station, at an altitude of 580 feet and opened with the line, serves also Castleton and Bradwell, both about 2½ miles distant. Castleton is noted for its ancient Peveril Castle (founded by William Peveril, the Norman adventurer) which was made famous by Sir Walter Scott's novel, and for its great caverns, the Speedwell, Peak, Treak Cliff and Blue John, which are open to the public. These are old lead ore mines, some of which have yielded the fabulous 'Blue John' fluorspar, the rarest and perhaps most beautiful of England's semi-precious stones, which could only be found in this region. The village is the centre of the High Peak region where old traditions and customs are still retained and the 'Old Religion' retains it dark secrets.

Further to the east, Bradwell, a village of old irregularly-placed houses, nestles in a valley of its own, with wild crags and overhanging rocks decorating the impressive scenic beauty which boasts the celebrated

Top
Hope station at the turn of the century, looking towards Dore as staff await the arrival of a 'down' train whilst the goods yard, beyond the footbridge, is a scene of activity.

Centre
Hope station, shorn of all Midland buildings and without a single platform seat, receives a diesel multiple unit on its way to Sheffield, 21 August 1984. View taken from the footbridge which remains.

Bottom
Hope village about c1910.

'Bagshawe Cavern' with its stalactites and crystalline columns. The village was once a centre for leadmining and smelting, lime manufacturing and hat-making.

Hope station was originally built on a different plan to the others in this area, with the station buildings and booking office on the road overbridge. It was opened with the line and continues to serve commuter and tourist alike although it lost its goods services from 20 April 1964. The station buildings were demolished in July 1970.

The Hope station of today is a graceless utilitarian set-up, comprising a bus-type windowless shelter, built of simulated stone and with a cast concrete roof, on both 'up' and 'down' platforms which are otherwise entirely lacking in facilities, with not even an old style station seat. The only redeeming feature is the elegant Midland lattice ironwork footbridge which straddles the line at the eastern end and not only affords access to each platform, but also provides a

Top
Hope valley, with the village in the centre of the picture, as it was on 22 August 1893 just before the Dore and Chinley line opened.

Centre
Official Midland Railway postcard depicting the Castle of Peveril of the Peak and the Peak Cavern, 2000 feet long, in the mouth of which ropes were made for over a century, taking advantage of the cavern's huge size and stable humidity conditions.

Below left
Stalactites make a fine display in the Treak Cliff Cavern, Castleton.

Below right
Visitors to the Speedwell Cavern travel by boat to view its many attractive sights.

57

footpath-crossing over the tracks. Attached to the strip lighting lamp post on each platform a modern sign proclaims the station's name, adding 'Trains to Sheffield' or 'Trains to Manchester' respectively.

Leaving Hope the line passes the branch to Earle's Cement Works and then swings in a loop to the north, following the River Noe as it passes between Win Hill (1,523 feet high) to the north and Lose Hill (1,563 feet high) to the south and then skirts the base of the unstable mass of sandstone and shale which is Mam Tor, the 'shivering mountain', on the heights of which is a sixteen-acre site covered with the remains of an Iron Age settlement.

Having twice crossed over the Noe, the railway runs into our next station at Edale (169 miles 14 chains), 820 feet above sea level and identical in most respects to the others, with platforms either side of the double track main line. Passenger traffic continues although goods facilities were withdrawn on 7 October 1963 and the station became an unstaffed halt from 7 September 1969.

Being immediately south of Kinder Scout, the highest hill in the Peak which rises to 2,088 feet, Edale is probably the most popular centre in the area for experienced walkers and climbers who ascend the many gritstone edges at all times of the year, with ski-ing an added attraction in the winter months.

Kinder Scout was the first area to which was applied the access provisions of the National Parks Act and Edale marks the southern end of the difficult Pennine Way walk which extends 250 miles from here to the Cheviot Hills. Here also is the Peak Park Board's warden centre, an information centre and a mountain rescue post, and the Rowland Cote youth hostel of the YHA which is one of the highest in England.

Edale village, more properly called Edale Chapel, is an extensive township of pretty gritstone houses and cottages which is surrounded by hamlets unusually bearing the name Booth, of which Nether Booth, Barber Booth and Upper Booth are the main ones, whilst other hamlets bear the names Oller Brook and Grinds Brook, which was the name of the hamlet before the

Top
The village of Bradwell nestling at the entrance to its dale.

Centre
Edale station in Midland days showing the goods dock.

Below
Edale station as a diesel multiple unit from Sheffield approaches, 13 July 1967.

name 'Edale' was chosen. The 300-year-old Nag's Head Inn, the local hostelry, has catered down the ages for the needs of both residents and visitors alike.

The village had 466 inhabitants in 1851 mainly engaged in agriculture and in the doubling of cotton in Lorenzo Christie's factory nearby which was worked by both water and steam power. The population was however in decline by the year 1900. The Duke of Devonshire is Lord of the Manor and owner of some 1,400 acres of land.

Leaving Edale station, in a little less than a mile the railway plunges into Cowburn tunnel (3,702 yards) which marks the exit from the Hope Valley and carries the line through the lower slopes of Brown Knoll (1,866 feet high) (Colburn Hill on the 1916 OS Map) to emerge from the western portal below Bowden Head, less than a mile from the triangular junction serving both Chinley and Buxton directions.

Cowburn tunnel, ninth longest in Britain, cost £270,246 to construct and the headings met on 18 June 1891 when the centre line was found to be a

Top left
View in 1955 looking east at a typical Midland signal box and signal at Norman's Bank between Edale and Cowburn tunnel.

Top right
A 'Jubilee' 4-6-0 heads an 'up' train into Edale station, 11 July 1957. The range of hills in the distance forms the obstacle which caused Cowburn tunnel to be built.

Centre
Edale station, looking towards Chinley, 13 July 1967.

Bottom
The viaduct over the river Noe, looking towards Edale, as the 1.45pm diesel multiple unit train from Manchester Piccadilly to Sheffield travels across, 20 May 1972.

mere one inch out and the horizontal lines met exactly! The summit of the Dore and Chinley line actually occurs inside the tunnel, some 913 yards from the eastern end and, after rising at a gradient of 1 in 100, falls at 1 in 150 towards Chinley. Only one permanent shaft was built which emerges at the side of the main bore. Work on that shaft began on 3 October 1888 and excavations then proceeded in each direction from its bottom, spoil being extracted by metal skips. At one time, before the headings met with the ends of the tunnel, water collected to a depth of 90 feet, and the tunnellers worked in diving bells.

Engineers for the whole of the line were Edward Parry, MICE of Nottingham and J. Somes Story, MICE of Derby. The contractor for the first 10½ miles was Thomas Oliver of Horsham, the last section at the Chinley end being contracted to J. P. Edwards of Chester.

Less than a mile from Cowburn we reach Chinley East Junction (168 miles 33 chains) where the line swings away via the South Junction to connect with Chapel-en-le-Frith, Peak Forest and Buxton (now freight only), and to the north towards Chinley station via Chinley North Junction, where we shall pick up the route in Chapter 5.

Top left
Kinder Downfall.

Top right
The eastern end of Cowburn tunnel and its typical Midland signals; the 'down' line signal, nearest the camera, has a white painted sighting board to enable train crews to see clearly the position of the signal arm.

Centre
Directors' tour on 10 August 1893 with the train on the 'up' line between Cowburn Tunnel East and Edale. The wagons carry contractor Thomas Oliver's initials and the engine is 0-4-2 saddletank *Cocker*, built originally in 1848 by Kitchen & Co for the Cockermouth and Workington Railway and converted to a tank engine in January 1886 by the LNWR at Crewe before eventually becoming a contractor's locomotive.

Bottom
Chinley North Junction showing 'Stanier' 2-8-0 48447 on an 'up' freight on the Dore line, 17 May 1952.

4
Through little Switzerland

Leaving Ambergate via the West Junction, the Midland's main route to Manchester ran along the eastern side of the A6 road, sandwiched between the former Cromford Canal to the right and the River Derwent to the left as it meanders along the valley floor.

The stretch of line from Ambergate as far as Rowsley was built by the Manchester, Buxton, Matlock and Midlands Junction Railway, and officially opened on 4 June 1849 between these two points although passenger and coal traffic did not commence until 20 August, other freight services commencing at the end of December.

The first station was Watstandwell Bridge, located originally some 21 chains to the north of the present one at the rear of the Derwent Hotel and at the northern end of Whatstandwell Tunnel (149 yards) and later became the location of goods operations when the new station was opened on 11 November 1894. It became plain 'Whatstandwell' from July 1896 and is still open, served by the branch line service to Matlock, although goods traffic ceased from 6 April 1964. The original station at Whatstandwell Bridge does not appear in the timetable for the line dated 'June 1st, 1852, and until further notice' but does appear in the Midland timetable for October 1853.

To the east the valley side rises up steeply through partial woodlands to Crich Chase and the village of Crich, already mentioned in Chapter 2, now home of the National Tramway

Previous page
A superb view of Ambergate station, looking north from the hillside above Toadmoor tunnel in the summer of 1911, as Midland 4-4-0 728 heads along the main line towards Whatstandwell.

Top
BR 'Britannia' Class 4-6-2 70021 *Morning Star* steams through No. 2 platform at Ambergate with an express from Manchester Central, 12 July 1958.

Centre
A number of roads through the Peak were subject to tolls and this view shows the old toll bar and toll house at Ambergate giving access to the road to Whatstandwell.

Bottom
A 'down' freight train near Ambergate *c*1930 headed by Kirtley double-framed 0-6-0 2579 and Johnson single frame 31XX series 0-6-0.

Museum which is situated in part of the extensive limestone quarries, whilst up on the heights of Crich Hill rises the tower of Crich Stand with its night-time revolving beacon light, the third such structure to be dedicated as a memorial to the fallen of the Sherwood Foresters Regiment, this one by General Sir H. L. Smith Dorrien, GCB, GCMG, DSO at a ceremony on Monday, 6 August 1923.

Top
Ex-Midland 4-4-0 331 heads northwards out of Ambergate with a 'down' stopping train in early LMS days.

Centre
The original Whatstandwell station, still in existence today, looking towards Whatstandwell tunnel. The second and present station can be seen just beyond. The Cromford canal lies beyond the supporting wall on the left.

Bottom left
Old Midland drinking fountain built into the supporting wall, where the first Whatstandwell 'up' platform was situated. It is inscribed 'WATSTANWELL' and dated '1861' in Roman numerals.

Bottom right
The second and present Whatstandwell station, looking towards Ambergate, 25 August 1952. All the station buildings were demolished in 1976 and the stonework used to build Hammersmith station platforms at the Midland Railway Centre. The track is now singled and a simple shelter forms the only accommodation.

The name 'Whatstandwell' is a quaint corruption of that derived from the Darley Abbey Charter at Belvoir which records an agreement in 1393 between Thomas, Abbot of Darley, and John de Stepul whereby the latter intended to construct a bridge at his own cost over the Derwent 'next to the house which Walter Stonewell had held of the convent, where no bridge had ever been constructed before'.

Top
Whatstandwell station and staff about 1907. The view was taken looking north.

Centre
The bridge over the Derwent at Whatstandwell, with the Derwent Hotel on the right and just beyond the entrance to the old station and former goods yard.

Bottom
A busy Whatstandwell goods yard looking towards the Ambergate *c*1907 as a 'down' freight train headed by 'Kirtley' 0-6-0 2376 passes an 'up' freight. A team of horses stand ready for work and two men adjust a tree trunk on a pair of road bogies.

Opposite the village, which has houses constructed of stone from the nearby quarries and which merge into the surrounding woods, and across the valley are the Shining Cliff woods, presented to the National Trust by Alderman J. G. Graves of Sheffield. Lea Hurst, the home of Florence Nightingale, lies near to the village, which she knew well as a young girl tending the local poor, sick and needy before answering the call to nursing. Her subsequent devoted service in the Crimea made her name a household word.

Beyond the village the line crosses the Derwent and reaches High Peak Junction (141 miles 24 chains) where the London & North Western Railway's Cromford and High Peak line formerly diverged on the left and meandered through woodlands to Cromford Goods wharf at the end of the Cromford Canal, before beginning its astonishing climb by means of rope-worked inclines operated by stationary engines to Whaley Bridge and the Peak Forest canal some 34 miles distant.

Top
Midland 4-4-0 727 heads a 'down' express through Whatstandwell in the summer of 1911.

Centre
Kirtley 0-6-0 864 crosses the original bridge over the Derwent, near High Peak Junction, with a freight train c1885.

Bottom
True Midland style – Deeley Compound 4-4-0 1019 heads a southbound express past High Peak Junction, whilst in the siding Kirtley 0-6-0 2418 engages in shunting – another scene from 1911.

Crossing the Derwent, the Midland enters Lea Wood tunnel (315 yards) and emerges to cross the Derwent again by means of a further bridge before arriving at Cromford. This was once a most charming station built about 1860, in the French style, allegedly to the designs of G. H. Stokes, son-in-law of Sir Joseph Paxton. In early days it was known as Cromford Bridge, had William Lees for stationmaster, with five passenger trains each way during weekdays, and a single train each way on Sundays, the latter calling at 9.45am northbound and at 7.15pm coming south. This frequency had only slightly increased a century later with an extra two trains in the week and three trains each way on Sundays.

Cromford village is renowned as the cradle of the cotton revolution for which credit must go to Sir Richard Arkwright, the one-time barber and itinerant wig-maker and thirteenth child of a Preston working man, who brought his inventive genius to Cromford and, in 1771, in partnership with Jedediah Strutt, founded Derbyshire's first water-powered cotton mill, adapting James Hargreaves' 'spinning Jenny' to produce spun-cotton, fine and strong enough to warp. This factory became the birthplace of mass production techniques and was a key to the Industrial Revolution.

Arkwright became so rich he was able, one Christmas, to give each of his ten children a gift of £10,000. His family mansion, Willersley Castle, which can be seen to the left as the line approaches Cromford, is now a Methodist guest house and retreat. Arkwright was buried in the village in St Mary's Church, which he had founded in 1792.

Top
Wagons being hauled by cable up the Sheep Pasture incline in the LNWR's Cromford and High Peak Railway from Cromford wharf which lies beyond the bridge carrying the road from Whatstandwell to Cromford. The Midland line lies in the valley beyond.

Centre
Ex-Midland 0-6-0 3379 enters Cromford station with a 'down' freight train.

Bottom
Cromford station on a summer afternoon in 1911 is the subject of this superb photograph as 'Deeley Compound' 4-4-0 1021 heads an 'up' express through the station without even a glance from the gentleman on the platform seat.

Other Cromford industries once included lead mining and smelting, the manufacture of red-lead and 'grinding and preparing calaminari (ie colour works) etc' which kept the population of 1,400 busily employed in the early 1840s, although a decline in the population occurred by the year 1900 when it fell to below 1,100.

Leaving Cromford the railway immediately enters Willersley Tunnel (764 yards) and then runs through a deep, rocky cutting before arriving at Matlock Bath (143 miles 73 chains) whose station was built for the opening of the line in the style of a Swiss chalet.

Matlock Bath and its immediate area was christened by Victorians 'Little Switzerland', its natural beauty being a somewhat miniature version of that enchanting country. However, prior to the year 1698, when warm spring-waters were found there, it was a place of little consequence. With that discovery a Bath House was built with a few rooms adjoining but with the increased fame of the waters, accommodation was improved. More springs were discovered there and a new road was opened linking through to the bridge in Old Matlock. 'The Bath' was truly opened up when Richard Arkwright Junior blasted a new entrance into Matlock Dale, near where his father had built his second mill in the year 1783. The development of Matlock Bath as a tourist attraction was thus assured and with the arrival

Top
Cromford station on the same day in 1911, looking south as a 'down' express headed by a 'Johnson' 2-4-0 passes through with a carriage on a truck at its rear.

Centre
Cromford village and pool as pictured in January 1985 – a scene little changed over the years.

Bottom
BR 'Standard' 2-10-0 92158 emerging from Willersley tunnel with a 'down' mineral train, 23 April 1965.

of the railway in 1849, providing much improved access, it became even more popular.

Terraced houses were built up the hill sides and fresh discoveries made in the original Roman and later-period leadmine workings of what are now the Rutland and Great Masson caverns. These were opened to the public and, added to the attractions of the petrifying well and the splendid rocky prominences of the Heights of Abraham and High Tor, soon made Matlock Bath a favourite resort. Further developments followed and today there are the 'Lovers Walk' riverside gardens, a mining museum, and a cable-car ride across the valley to the Heights of Abraham where visitors can view the scene from the Victoria Prospect Tower, whilst in late summer each year a week of 'Venetian Lights', with illuminations along the

Top
Matlock Bath in July 1889, as captured by the Midland's own photographer.

Centre
Matlock Bath station *c*1878 with a Kirtley 890 Class 2-4-0 (No. 92 or 72) at the head of a train of early four- and six-wheeled carriages.

Bottom
The arrival for a day's picnic at Matlock Bath station in 1930 – an excursion from St Pancras to Matlock stands ready to complete its journey hauled by ex-Midland 'Compound' 4-4-0 1042 while the day trippers make their way under the railway to ascend High Tor.

Top left
Richard Arkwright's Masson Mill established in 1769, at the entrance to Matlock Bath dale from Cromford.

Top right
Excursion leaflet of 1864 advertising a trip from the Leeds area to taste the delights of Matlock and Matlock Bath plus the twin attractions of Chatsworth House and Haddon Hall.

Bottom
Matlock Bath seen from the Heights of Jacob, 12 June 1913. John Smedley's Riber Castle can be seen on top of the hill to the right and below it, in the valley, the Midland station.

river and illuminated boats, attracts thousands of visitors.

Matlock Bath station was closed to goods traffic from 6 April 1964 and to passengers from 6 March 1967, only to be re-opened as an unstaffed halt on 27 May 1972 when the first train, an excursion from Burton-on-Trent, arrived behind Class 47 Brush diesel-electric locomotive No. D1744.

The station now has a one class only diesel multiple unit service to and from Derby with twelve trains each way Mondays-Fridays, eight on Saturdays and two on Sundays. At the time of writing, a new diesel railcar of Class 150 was running trials under the title 'The Matlock Sprinter'.

Leaving Matlock Bath station the line immediately plunges into three tunnels which pierce the foot of High Tor cliffs and which are, respectively, 321, 58 and 378 yards long. Being cut through limestone, these have given much cause for careful maintenance over the years and extensive lining and re-lining exercises have been undertaken to keep them open. Between Nos. 1A and 2 tunnels the railway briefly emerges into daylight and passengers may catch a glimpse of the gorge with the River Derwent below before the train plunges again into darkness.

The line eventually emerges on to a ledge above the river which it crosses by means of an iron-girder bridge and, passing through the 126-yard Holt Lane tunnel, arrives in Matlock station, which is precisely 145 miles from St Pancras.

Lovers Walks & River Derwent, Matlock Bath.

Matlock Bridge

Opposite page:– top
Street scene in Matlock Bath, 12 June 1913, looking towards Matlock with the Victoria Prospect tower on the Heights of Abraham top centre. An open-topped tourer has the main street to itself.

Opposite Centre
Lover's Walk, a favourite courting spot in Matlock Bath beside the Derwent, momentarily taken over by three white-smocked girls with hoops, beside the ferry crossing.

Opposite Bottom
The bridge which carries the Midland main line over the Derwent as it approaches Matlock, or to give it its earlier name, 'Matlock Bridge'.

This page:– top
Ex-Midland 'Compound' 4-4-0 1044 makes a smoky exit from High Tor tunnels with a 'down' express before the Second World War.

Centre
Paxton's Matlock station buildings as they appear today. The station is now unstaffed.

Bottom
Crown Square, Matlock Bridge, with a Matlock Steep Cable Tramway car at the lower terminus. This tramway carried passengers up the very steep Bank Road as far as Rutland Street. It was the steepest in the world with a gradient of 1 in 5½ and operated from 1893 to 1927.

The tram shelter and clock tower were built in 1899. Note horse-drawn omnibuses on the left.

Known by the Midland as 'Matlock Bridge' until 1 July 1905 it was renamed 'Matlock' after pressure from the local populace who wished to accord the town its rightful title as an ancient centre. The station closed to goods traffic from 4 September 1972 but remains open mainly for commuter and tourist traffic though, to the great regret of many, it now marks the end of this once magnificent Midland route to Manchester.

Both the station and stationmaster's house, completed in 1850, were designed by Sir Joseph Paxton, famous for his design of the Crystal Palace. Opened on a Saturday, by the following morning some despicable thief had removed all the lead from the roof of the station buildings!

Matlock, situated at the convergence of two valleys which descend from Tansley Moor and at the meeting point of five roads, is today a busy but pleasant place, its main problem being traffic jams which, despite its having been widened on one side in 1903, still occur on the sixteenth-century bridge over the Derwent which joins the two halves of the town.

CROWN SQUARE, MATLOCK.

Matlock Bank, which rises to the east of the railway, was developed by John Smedley, Hosiery Manufacturer, who, having been cured of a health breakdown on visiting a spa, was anxious that others should benefit. After experiments with his workpeople at Lea Mills the beginnings of Smedley's Hydro, in the shape of a small house purchased in 1852, resulted eventually in the erection of the magnificent hydropathic establishment which, in 1958, became the headquarters of Derbyshire County Council.

From the fortune made by this activity John Smedley built Riber Castle, clearly visible at the top of a nearby hill, where he died in the year 1874. It is now the site of a wildlife park and zoo.

The Midland line beyond Matlock, which is now dismantled as far as Peak Forest Junction, is currently the subject of extremely ambitious plans by Peak Rail Ltd to re-open the next sixteen miles which contains no less than seven major tunnels and two enormous viaducts along its twisting and winding route.

Half-a-mile beyond the station are the huge Cawdor Quarries, still in use, which have, via the Midland Railway, provided stone for Hyde Park Corner, the Thames Embankment and a thousand other places and, after crossing the Derwent once, the line soon ran into Darley Dale station, although the nearest village is called Church Town, its ancient remains dating back to Roman times. The famous 'Darley Yew Tree', with a trunk 33-feet-round and bound with iron hoops, is calculated to be between seven and nine hundred years old and stands in the graveyard of St Helen's Church which has many ancient Saxon remains, also a twelve-panel south transept window by Burne-Jones and William Morris depicting 'The Song of Solomon', erected in memory of Raphael Gillman who died in 1860 aged ninety years.

Top
L.M.S. 2-6-0 42902 stands ready to depart from Matlock station with an 'up' stopping train, August 1959.

Centre
Group of pupils posing by the Whitworth monument and Institute at Darley Dale in 1917.

Bottom
St Helen's church and school at Darley Dale in 1907.

MANCHESTER, BUXTON, MATLOCK, & MIDLANDS JUNCTION RAILWAY.

June 1st, 1852, and until further Notice.

LEAVE	IN CONNEXION WITH TRAINS	From DERBY	From LEEDS and the North. From DERBY, NOTTINGHAM, BIRMINGHAM, &c.	From LEEDS and the North. From LONDON, DERBY, NOTTINGHAM, LINCOLN, BIRMINGHAM, &c.	From LEEDS and the North. From LONDON, DERBY, NOTTINGHAM, LINCOLN, BIRMINGHAM, &c.	From LONDON, DERBY, NOTTINGHAM, BIRMINGHAM, &c.	From LEEDS and the North. From LONDON DERBY, NOTTINGHAM, &c.	SUNDAY TRAINS.
		A.M.	A.M.	P.M.	P.M.	P.M.	P.M.	A.M.
DERBY - - -		7.45	9.30	12.55	3.50	6. 0	9. 0	9. 0
Ambergate - -		8.20	10. 8	1.25	4.20	6.55	9.25	9.35
Cromford - -		8.34	10.22	1.39	4.34	7. 9	9.39	9.49
Matlock Bath -		8.37	10.25	1.42	4.37	7.12	9.42	9.52
Matlock Bridge		8.40	10.28	1.45	4.40	7.15	9.45	9.55
Darley - - -		8.45	10.33	1.50	4.45	7.20	9.50	10. 0
Rowsley Arrive		8.50	10.38	1.55	4.50	7.25	9.55	10. 5

LEAVE	IN CONNEXION WITH TRAINS	To DERBY, LONDON, &c.	To LEEDS and the North. To DERBY, LONDON, NOTTINGHAM, LINCOLN, BIRMINGHAM, &c.	To DERBY, LONDON, &c.	To LEEDS and the North. To DERBY, LONDON, NOTTINGHAM, LINCOLN, BIRMINGHAM, &c.	To LEEDS and the North. To DERBY, BIRMINGHAM, &c., and Express to LONDON.	To LEEDS and the North. To DERBY, NOTTINGHAM, &c.	To LEEDS and the North. To DERBY, LONDON, BIRMINGHAM, &c.	SUNDAY TRAINS.
		A.M.	A.M.	P.M.	P.M.	P.M.	P.M.		P.M.
Rowsley - - -		9.15	11. 15	2.50	5. 0	6.15	8. 40		7. 0
DARLEY - - -		9.20	11.20	2.55	5. 5	6.20	8. 45		7. 5
MATLOCK BRIDGE		9.25	11.25	3. 0	5.10	6.25	8. 50		7.10
MATLOCK BATH -		9.28	11.28	3. 3	5.13	6.28	8. 53		7.13
CROMFORD - - -		9.30	11.30	3. 5	5.15	6.30	8. 55		7.15
Ambergate - -		9.45	11.45	3.20	5.27	6.45	9. 10		7.27
DERBY Arrive		10.45	12.15	3.55	6. 5	8. 0	10.47		8. 5

N.B. At the Rowsley Station, Omnibuses to and from Chatsworth, Bakewell and Haddon, meet the Trains:—Fare, 6d. each.

Post-Horses and Conveyances always in readiness.

Printed by Wm. Bemrose & Son, Derby.

Also buried at Darley Dale is the man largely responsible for mechanising this world who, in the year 1841, introduced a standard system of screw-threads and accurate measuring devices and later made a number of other improvements in the engineering sphere. He was Joseph Whitworth, born in Stockport in 1803, who had worked in his uncle's cotton mill at fourteen, ran away to Manchester and then later to London and, whilst living frugally and working for Maudslay 'invented' the true-plane and followed with many more ingenious inventions. His contributions changed engineering thinking and the Midland Railway was among some undertakings to take on board and utilise the new standards in their manufacture of locomotives and rolling-stock.

Top
Manchester, Buxton, Matlock and Midlands Junction Railway timetable of 1852.

Centre
'Jubilee' Class 4-6-0 45659 *Drake* passes Darley Dale with the 'up' *Palatine* express c1959. The footbridge is now at the Midland Railway Centre.

Bottom
'Jubilee' 45557 *New Brunswick* heads an 'up' express through Darley Dale while a porter sorts parcels on the 'down' platform c1959.

The local quarry provided stone for St George's Hall, Liverpool, and for its lions, each weighing six tons, which were fashioned here. It is said that Whitworth more than recouped the cost of the nearby Stancliffe Hall Estate, in which the quarry lies, by this one outstanding sale! He lived the last fifteen years of his life at Stancliffe Hall and died in the year 1887. A memorial statue stands beside the A6 road at Darley Dale near to the Whitworth Institute which he had founded, along with a Winter Garden built on the site of an old quarry. A hospital was later founded here in his memory by his wife.

The station at Darley Dale (147 miles 14 chains), built in Gothic style and opened with the line on 20 August 1849, was originally called Darley, 'Dale' being added from 1 October 1890.

Services over the years varied but little, with an average of six local trains in each direction on weekdays and three on Sundays. The station closed to goods traffic on 6 April 1964 and completely on 6 March 1967. The buildings remain and are used for industrial purposes.

Darley Dale is a scattered rural township with a centre more properly named Church Town and a five-arch stone bridge over the Derwent leading to Darley Bridge, formerly called Bridge Town, whilst to the east of the main road and to the north lies Two Dales, Darley Hillside and Northwood. In 1851 there were nearly 1,400 inhabitants but the population had doubled by the turn of the century, largely due to the coming of the

Top
The original goods yard at Rowsley *c*1870 with the first engine shed in the centre distance. One Kirtley locomotive is shunting on the right and another is outside the shed. Beyond the overbridge stands the MBM&MJR station on the original alignment of that line, whilst the new Midland line and station are on the extreme left.

Centre
Rowsley second locomotive shed built on part of the goods yard, with engines standing on the former MB&MJR main line and the second Rowsley station on the extreme left.

Bottom
The third Rowsley engine shed, 13 April 1958, built alongside the extensive sidings. Two snowploughs are ready for duty and engines 'on shed' include an ex-North London 0-6-0 tank, a 'Crab' 2-6-0, a 'Fairbairn' 2-6-4 tank, a Class 4F 0-6-0 and Class 3F 0-6-0 tender and tank engines.

railway and development of local industries. Some infill housing has been built during the present century and the population has now swelled to around 6,500.

The railway then swung to the north-east on its old route, and in a short distance reached the now derelict site of the once thriving Rowsley marshalling yard, with its north and south sidings and engine sheds.

The original MBM&MJR marshalling yard and engine shed at Rowsley were further to the north, just south of the overbridge which carried the main road over the original line of railway, and adjacent to the first Rowsley station building which was designed by Sir Joseph Paxton and built by the company in the year 1849. Still in existence, the old station building is of stone with a characteristic gabled roof, three tall stone chimneys and mullion windows. It was brought into use with the opening of the line and was not replaced until 1 August 1862 when the new station was opened on a new alignment of the extension to Hassop which veers away to the north-west. The older building then became a goods station at the end of a short branch off the new main line which terminated 149 miles 39 chains from St Pancras.

A new four-road engine shed, constructed by Messrs E. Wood at a cost of £2,561, was opened late in 1879 on the same site. A turntable was added in 1882 and by then the stud of locomotives had increased to cover banking duties to the north as far as Peak Forest summit, and for shunting work in the sidings. New shed accommodation was later provided by the LMSR in 1923 about a mile further south, beside the new marshalling yard which was developed quickly following the initial interchange of

Top
Stranger on a northbound freight approaching Rowsley station, September 1958. BR Class 9F 2-10-0 92143 was an Eastern Region engine for all its life and appears here well out of its territory.

Centre
'Jubilee' Class 4-6-0 45652 *Hawke* enters Rowsley station with a 'down' express for Manchester *c*1960.

Bottom
Rowsley station in happier Midland days in September 1903, looking south with the second engine shed clearly visible to the left. Passengers wait on the platform seats beneath the cast-iron glass-covered awning, and milk churns await collection.

traffic with the London & North Western Railway at Buxton, when that route opened on 1 June 1863, and further still with the opening of the Midland's through route to Manchester in 1867.

Traffic originating from Lancashire and beyond was sorted here for destinations to London, the East Midlands and East Anglia and, from Derby, to the west, and was also sorted for destinations to the north. Freight trains were assisted up the heavy gradients to Peak Forest by locomotives from Rowsley shed. At one time the yard was handling over ten thousand wagon-loads weekly but in April 1964, with ever-diminishing traffic and a gradual run-down of the route, the yard closed and on the 27th of that month the locomotive depot became a stabling point only, remaining open for a further year or so merely to service visiting engines.

The new station at Rowsley was built on a curve of line carrying the railway into the heart of the Wye valley on a new route, authorised by Act of Parliament dated 25 May 1860. Work on this line, linking Rowsley with Buxton, began on 4 September of the same year in the cutting at the southern end of Haddon tunnel and its construction was undoubtedly one of the most notable engineering achievements of its decade, encountering, during operations, rocky heights and subterranean rivers.

The station, 149 miles 36 chains from St Pancras, consisted of an accommodation building on the 'up' side with glass canopied roofs over both 'up' and 'down' platforms, the latter connected by means of a subway and, to complete the scene, a goods and cattle dock at the south end of the 'up' platform. It opened for traffic on 1 August 1862 to permit use of the extension as far as Hassop, by then complete. Services at the time were seven trains daily each way with two on Sundays, with fares from Derby of

3s 6d (17½p) First Class; 2s 6d (12½p) Second Class; and 2s 0½d (10p) by Government trains. Omnibuses were provided to and from Chatsworth House for all trains excepting the early morning ones in either direction. One could book an ordinary Second Class ticket to London for £1 with a return costing £1.10s 0d (£1.50p). A horse would cost £3.14s 0d (£3.70p) for the same distance; a private carriage (carried by carriage-truck) £2.15s 6d (£2.77½p); and a dog 3s 0d (15p).

Rowsley was the main station for visitors to Chatsworth House, perhaps the finest of England's country houses, a noble residence of the Cavendish family, the Dukes of Devonshire. Built in the late seventeenth century in Palladian style, with a deer park ten miles in circumference, laid out by 'Capability' Brown, it also boasts magnificent gardens, water cascades and the great Emperor Fountain forcing a giant plume of water some 290 feet into the air. Chatsworth today remains a treasure house of fine furniture, paintings, tapestries, porcelain and other works of art and is open to the public each year from March to early October.

Rowsley, at the meeting of the Derwent and Wye, is a small village whose chief features are its bridge over the Derwent and the nearby famous Peacock Hotel, originally built as a manor house in 1652 by John Stevenson, Agent to Grace, Lady Manners, with his name and the date over the doorway. Above the porch is a fine stone peacock, crest of the Manners' family, accounting for the inn's present name, and today it is a favourite resort for travellers, anglers and tourists alike. Both Landseer the artist, and Longfellow the poet have stayed within its walls.

Over the bridge, a row of identical railway workers' cottages remind us of the former importance of the place in the Midland Railway's network.

Top
Midland official carriage print depicting Chatsworth House in all its grandeur.

Bottom
Rowsley station, looking north in September 1903. Note the cattle dock with inside-keyed track still in situ and a horse and carriage awaiting the arrival of the 'up' train.

5
In the heart of the Peak

Leaving Rowsley station, the track first passed over the Bakewell road by a bridge, whose last renewal was in 1965 (only two years before the line closed, when it was quickly demolished) and then almost immediately over the Derwent before entering Haddon Tunnel (1058 yards) which carried the line out of sight beneath the Duke of Rutland's estate and country house, Haddon Hall. However, because it was to be only slightly below ground level, the tunnel was constructed mainly by the 'cut and cover' method, only part of it actually being bored. It is ventilated by five shafts of which the deepest is only 12 feet, while the largest occupies the whole 33-feet width of the tunnel. The headings met on 11 March 1861, but on 2 July of the same year part of it collapsed. Four men were killed outright and one was so seriously injured that he died the following day. £100 was paid to the dependants of each man as compensation for the loss of the family bread winner.

Haddon Hall, whilst not of the same size as Chatsworth, is nevertheless a charming mansion and stands on a spot which has been home for both the Vernon family, who came there in the twelfth century, and the family of the current owners, the Dukes of Rutland who succeeded to the title in the sixteenth century. Mostly built about 1370, it has remnants of thirteenth-century stonework in its ancient chapel and some fifteenth-century wall paintings, whilst the house is a magnificently preserved example of medieval architecture with its Banqueting Hall, Minstrel Gallery, Tudor kitchens and dining rooms, State Apartments and a 110-feet-long Gallery. In an ante-room is Dorothy Vernon's door through which, as heiress to the estate, she

Previous page
Ex-Midland 2-4-0 84 double-heading a Class 4F 0-6-0 bursts out of Great Rocks Tunnel in a display of sheer power *c*1930.

Top
The terrace and steps at Haddon Hall, scene of Dorothy Vernon's romantic elopement with Sir John Manners.

Centre
Bakewell station and goods yard looking south, 9 July 1957. The town lies about half-a-mile away to the right.

Bottom
Midland period scene at Bakewell, 30 September 1903, looking south as passengers await the arrival of a 'down' stopping train.

eloped with Sir John Manners to Belvoir Castle and thus linked the family's future history with the Dukes of Rutland.

The railway emerged from Haddon Tunnel to run along the hillside, by now 100 feet above the Wye, and entered the next station at Bakewell where a location was chosen on a hill overlooking the town centre. With an imposing, and still existing, main accommodation block in stone situated on the 'down' platform, and a matching stone curtain wall on the 'up', both of which once had elaborate glass canopies, the buildings were basically identical in design with those at Rowsley, except that here a curtain wall was built to provide protection and to screen off the main road which, having crossed the line on a rising gradient towards the southern end of the station, passes behind the curtain wall at the top of an earth bank.

Beyond the main building an extensive goods yard catered for local traffic and offered usual facilities for coal merchants by way of coal offices and stacking compounds adjacent to the unloading track.

The station opened on 1 August 1862 and passenger traffic ceased on 6 March 1967.

In the 1850s and 1860s, when such travel was very limited, it was possible to obtain a Third Class ticket in order to travel to Bakewell Market from Buxton and intermediate stations by the 12.40pm from Buxton, returning on the 4.46pm train which also stopped at Longstone on Fridays only to set down passengers.

Bakewell, which derives its name from 'Badeca's Well', is a pleasant market town, despite a recently instituted one-way traffic system designed to cope with the influx of motor vehicles which bring visitors to savour its delights, amongst which are the famous Bakewell Puddings or Tarts which were originated in the

Top
Bakewell station viewed from the road overbridge, looking north as LMS Class 4F 0-6-0 44172 passes through 'light engine', 23 June 1961.

Centre
A train load of timber from Oxford for the church roof waits to be unloaded at Bakewell goods yard in 1906.

Bottom
The 'Rutland Arms', Bakewell, where the famous puddings originated as a result of a parlour maid's misinterpretation of instructions.

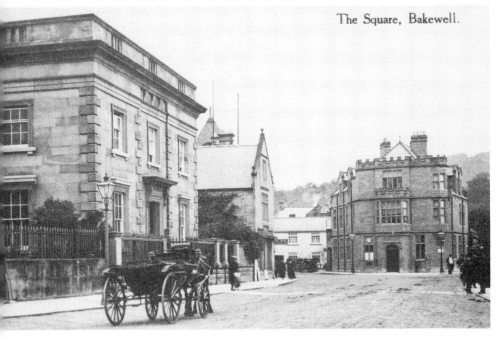

The Square, Bakewell.

Top
The town square at Bakewell *c*1906 with an open carriage awaiting hire outside the bank.

Centre
'Up' freight headed by Class 4F 0-6-0 44545 approaches Bakewell *c*1960.

Bottom
A 'down' empty coaching stock train passes the remains of Hassop Station, 23 June 1961, with Class 8F 2-8-0 48770 of Cricklewood shed in charge.

Rutland Arms Hotel by a kitchen maid who, happily for us, totally misunderstood her instructions way back in 1859!

Buildings of note include the seventeenth-century Market House of the Manners family which stands in Bridge Street, now a Peak National Park Information Centre, Bagshaw Hall which stands to the west of the church and dates from 1686, an ancient free school founded in 1636 by Grace, Lady Manners, and the Duke of Rutland's Bath House of 1697 which contains one of the town's two chalybeate wells.

The town is home for some 4,000 people, almost double the population of the 1850s.

The church, dedicated to All Saints, was one of the only two in Derbyshire with two priests at the time of the Domesday Book. It stands in the valley close to the river Wye and was founded in Anglo-Saxon times but rebuilt entirely by the Normans in the shape of a cross, to which an elegant octagonal-shaped spire was added in the middle of the last century to replace an earlier one.

An Anglian cross shaft in the churchyard dates from the eighth century and is decorated with scenes from the life of Christ, whilst the thirteenth-century Vernon chapel contains monuments to the Vernons, Manners and Foljambes.

At the west end of the churchyard is a stone memorial to one, John Dale, whose 'rambling remains' were laid to rest beside his two wives in April 1757, in his 86th year. His tombstone epitaph begins:

This thing in life might cause some jealousy
Here all three lie together lovingly

and ends:

A period's come to all their toylsome lives:
The good man's quiet – still are both his
*   wives.*

Beyond the church the one-time Priest's House is now a museum.

The five-arch bridge over the Wye

to the north-east of the town dates
from about 1300, whilst upstream
Holmes Bridge, a narrow stone
structure, was erected in 1664 to give
access to Holme Hall itself built some
time earlier in 1626.

From Bakewell the line ran in a
west-north-westerly direction towards
Buxton, and Ruskin sourly commented
when it was first opened: 'That valley
where you might expect to catch the
sight of Pan, Apollo and the Muses, is
now desecrated in order that a Buxton
fool may be able to find himself in
Bakewell at the end of twelve minutes,
and vice versa!'

Observing the effect of the Midland
line in a more objective manner today,
one cannot but disagree with Ruskin's
sentiments, for the construction of the
railway opened up many of the more
remote and picturesque parts of this
area of Derbyshire. Travelling by train
through these beautiful dales, and
using the facilities so provided to visit
the remote yet idyllically beautiful
spots, opened up a prospect of nature
denied to so many destined to labour
in the dreary and unlovely
manufacturing towns and cities that
surrounded the area in the nineteenth
and early twentieth centuries.

On leaving Bakewell, in less than a
mile the line reached Hassop, a
boarding point regularly used by the
Dukes of Devonshire, for the station
was the nearest to Chatsworth House.
The original intended route of the
MBM&MJR line north of Rowsley lay
through part of Chatsworth Park but
the Duke resisted the scheme and by
the time he realised the value of
having a railway near at hand and
offered his co-operation to the
Midland, it was 1865 and too late to
change the line of railway.

However, Hassop station was
provided as a compromise, but it is
almost two miles from the village of
that name and a mile or so from
Hassop Hall, the residence of a branch
of the Eyre family who held their
house against the Parliamentarians in
December 1643.

Top
The First World War scene at Hassop as
soldiers of the Royal Army Medical Corps
de-train with their horses and equipment.

Centre
Hassop station buildings on the 'up' side
minus its canopy, as it appears today in use
as industrial premises.

Bottom
The tree-lined village street of Hassop; the
few buildings include the 'Eyre Arms'. The
station lies a mile away to the left.

The little township was once noted for its leadmines which were called 'The Brightside', 'Backdale', 'Harrybruce', 'Waterhole' and 'Whitecoe' and were all still active in the middle of the nineteenth century.

Hassop station (153 miles 65 chains) opened with the first section of line on 1 August 1862, but it was an early casualty so far as passenger traffic was concerned, closing on 17 August 1942, although goods traffic continued until 5 October 1964. The main station building is still intact and in use as industrial premises, but the platforms are gone and the nearby stationmaster's house is derelict.

In a little over a mile the line entered Longstone station (155 miles 13 chains) which was also the station for Ashford-in-the-Water. It was, for once, quite near to the attractive and well-kept villages of Great Longstone and Little Longstone, which lie less than half-a-mile apart on the same road, and was renamed 'Great Longstone for Ashford' from the October 1913 timetable.

The style of the main building, which still stands on the 'down' platform, was intended to match nearby Thornbridge Hall, with its leaded glass windows and covered porch on the platform, whilst on the 'up' platform a simple, stone-built shelter was provided. Passenger services were discontinued on 10 September 1962.

Great Longstone is a pleasing settlement lying under Longstone Edge, a gritstone ridge over three miles long which rises to 1,300 feet in height. The village has a manor house, an inn dedicated to the cobbler's saint, St Crispin, an eighteenth-century red brick Hall with origins dating back to the fourteenth century and for generations the home of the Wright family, and the church of St Giles which dates back to the thirteenth century. The village cross dates back to an earlier century when Flemish weavers first settled there.

Little Longstone is a smaller village

Top
A difficult scene to capture for the photographer of the period – a moving express headed by Midland 4-4-0 1673 near Hassop c1898.

Centre
The station at 'Great Longstone for Ashford' as it appeared on 15 May 1953.

Bottom
A peaceful summer scene in Great Longstone village in August 1984 – such quiet places can still be found today!

along the road towards Monsal Head, with fine houses, well preserved village stocks, and a twin gabled seventeeth-century manor house, once home of the Longsdons of whom James was barmaster of the 'High Peak Hundred'.

Ashford-in-the-Water, also served by the station, lies in the beautiful Wye valley, and is a place of great charm, retaining many of its old customs such a well dressings on Trinity Sunday, the ringing every evening of the Curfew bell, and the Pancake bell on Shrove Tueday. Here also were the touching reminders of the ceremony of making garlands with paper ribbons which were hung in Holy Trinity church in memory of maidens who died unwed, and which carried their names and ages together with an epitaph verse, one of which was:

Be always ready, no time delay,
I in my youth was called away:
Great grief to those that's left behind,
But I hope I'm great joy to find
Ann Swindel
Aged 22 years   Dec 9th, 1798

The village is renowned, too, for its fine seventeenth-century Sheepwash Bridge with its fold still used for that purpose, and also for its black marble, widely used throughout the country for ornaments and tombstones, whose discovery and use we owe to Henry Watson of Bakewell, a son of Samuel Watson of Heanor who was responsible for much of the fine carving at Chatsworth House.

The line now ran through Headstone Tunnel (533 yards) which burrows beneath Little Longstone, and emerged almost directly onto Headstone Viaduct (usually incorrectly referred to as Monsal Dale Viaduct) with a view of the valley which is at once breathtaking and awe-inspiring.

Top
A Manchester to Derby express near Great Longstone headed by LMS 'Compound' 4-4-0 1046. Great Longstone was known for its rhododendrons and its topiary, with bushes trimmed to represent people and animals.

Centre
LMS 'Compound' 4-4-0 1050 heads north out of Headstones tunnel on to the viaduct in Monsal Dale in 1926 hauling an express train of almost new LMS stock.

Bottom
A superb photograph looking down on Headstones viaduct over the Derwent as Midland Class 4F 0-6-0 44026 (the last of the class built by the Midland at Derby Works) heads south with a mixed freight train, 15 May 1953.

The viaduct, 300 feet long, is carried on five stone arches, each 50 feet in span, at a height of some 40 feet above the Wye below, as the river curves in a broad sweep round Putty Hill and passes from beautiful Monsal Dale, on the left, to the broad valley which curves northwards and leads towards the source of the river on the moors above Buxton. As the line sweeps onwards, both railway and river run interlaced all the way to Buxton as the river passes through an exceptionally scenic and picturesque succession of valleys from the streams that feed its source.

Building of the viaduct was in hand by 1861 and the rocky landing from which it springs was built of waste material from the tunnel through which the line has just passed and the short cutting which immediately precedes the viaduct. Slippage began to occur at this point in the early part of this century and during 1907 and 1908 extensive work was carried out to stabilise both the embankment heading and the viaduct.

A popular picnic spot is Headstones Head, at the summit of the road out of the valley, which has for over a century provided a point from which to view the unparalleled beauty stretched out below, whilst sustenance is near at hand in the form of a refreshment room, and the adjacent Bull's Head Inn where many thousands of visitors who annually visit the spot may replenish their energies.

Imagine how this view would have been marred had the Lancashire, Derbyshire and East Coast Railway carried out their plan to cross the valley and the Midland main line on a massive viaduct some 300 feet high as part of their route to Lancashire! Had it been built this would have been the tallest structure of its kind in the country.

After leaving the viaduct and passing through a short cutting, the line of railway ran along the hillside forming the west side of Upper Dale and shortly arrived at Monsal Dale station (156 miles 46 chains), built to serve the villages of Upperdale and Cressbrook with its cotton mills. The mills were once owned by William Newton (1750-1830), the carpenter poet who was nicknamed 'Minstrel of the Peak'. He was largely self-taught, taking opportunities presented by his woodworking in halls and mansions where he worked. He eventually

became machinery carpenter at a cotton mill in Monsal Dale and in later years rose in the world and took on the Cressbrook Mills which flourished under his enlightened management. The mills, of which the first was built by Arkwright in 1779, were called Little Mill, Old Mill and Big Mill. The latter has a clock dated 1837 and a bell tower to call employees to work, and is a handsome building in yellow stucco with a high-pitched roof like a Georgian palace. Old Mill stands on the site of the original building, which was at one time used as a peppermint distillery using wild mint from the hillsides and was burnt down about 1790.

Monsal Dale station, opened 1 September 1866, perched on the hillside astride the line with the 'down' platform securely founded on rock and built of stone, whilst the 'up' platform, now demolished, stood on top of wooden piles driven into the hillside to provide support for the platform timbers. There were no buildings on this platform except the lone signal box on the hillside at the north end of the 'up' platform to control the goods sidings which consisted of a single loop alongside the 'down' line, plus the later addition of a shunting neck with access from both 'up' and 'down'

Opposite top
Another view of Headstones viaduct, this time looking to the west as the Midland express from Manchester heads south *c*1908.

Opposite centre
Vantage point at Monsal Dale Head! Popular for picnics with the nearby 'Bull's Head Inn' and unparalleled views down the dale.

Opposite bottom
The awe-inspiring view from Monsal Dale Head looking northwards up the valley. The Midland railway line can be seen clearly on the left with Monsal Dale station just beyond the cutting, and the mouth of Cressbrook tunnel a little further north.

Top
Official Midland photograph of Monsal Dale station looking north on 20 April 1911. Access was by means of a steep road out of the valley below. The station approach is on the left of the picture.

Centre
'Jubilee' 4-6-0 45629 *Straits Settlements*, heads through Monsal Dale station hauling an express for Manchester.

Bottom
Buxton branch train at Miller's Dale station headed by ex-Midland 0-4-4 tank 1421 waits to take up passengers from the main-line train for Manchester which has called at the platform opposite, 24 June 1933.

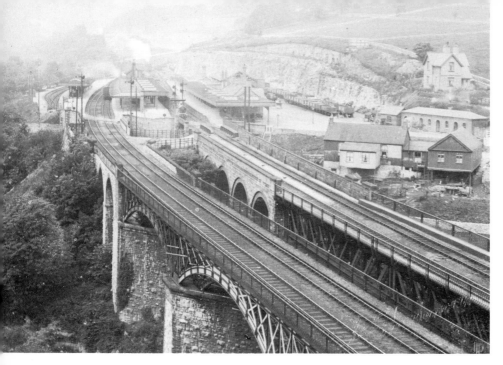

tracks. The original box stood at the north end of the 'down' platform and was moved to permit the latter alterations to take place.

The station building, on the 'down' side (parts of which came from Evesham), comprised a wooden booking office and waiting room plus the usual facilities. Services in Midland days numbered seven trains each way on weekdays plus one train which stopped only on its way south to set down passengers from beyond Marple, one which stopped to pick up passengers travelling beyond Chinley, and another which stopped to set down from London and/or pick up for Stockport and Manchester. Only two trains each way served the station on Sundays. By 1944 services had been cut to four trains each way on weekdays with no service on Sundays. The station was closed from 10 August 1959.

From Monsal Dale the line continued curving slightly towards the east and entered Cressbrook tunnel (471 yards) and 11 chains further on Litton tunnel (515 yards). Between the two, a secluded part of the Wye with no road access, suddenly burst on the rail traveller's view with the sheer precipices of Bull Tor and Eagle Tor rising above and the overhanging woods and shining waters of the river below. This brief scene was, for many railway travellers, one of the supremely beautiful and memorable vistas on the Midland line to Manchester and the location bears the charming name of 'Water-cum-Jolie'.

Both these tunnels were driven through solid rock, and Litton tunnel was unlined until the year 1880. Neither had ventilating shafts and both were cut on a curve to accommodate changes in alignment

Top
Looking north at Miller's Dale station. This view shows clearly the scale of civil engineering necessary to establish the station and twin viaducts. The goods and coal yards, with offices, are on the right of the picture. The card from which this view was taken is postmarked 31 December 1909.

Centre
This view of Miller's Dale station with the village below was taken by the Midland's photographer on 11 May 1910 and shows the twin double-track viaducts over the dale. Down below is the 'Station Hotel', kept by mine host George Starling.

Bottom
LMS 'Compound' 4-4-0 41192 approaching Miller's Dale with a Manchester Central to Derby stopping train, 4 September 1955.

Top
Part of the attractive Miller's Dale village in a picturesque setting beside the river Wye.

Centre
Tideswell village in 1904. The message on the postcard reads 'Derbyshire again this weekend. Just laying in supplies' – obviously written by someone who thoroughly enjoyed the Peak scenery.

Bottom
Samuel Slack, the celebrated Tideswell bass singer.

necessary to suit the surrounding hillsides which the line traversed. The railway here is rising on a 1 in 100 gradient (that is, each 100-foot-length of track sees a rise of one foot in its altitude above sea level), and this particular gradient commenced at the north end of Monsal Dale station and continued until nearing the next great engineering structure in the shape of the twin viaducts over which the line crossed the Wye again in its approaches to Millers Dale station.

In the beginning a single twin-track viaduct was built but operational requirements eventually dictated that a parallel second viaduct be built on the north side, and this was completed and opened on 20 August 1905. Construction had begun some two years earlier and the massive iron girders and arch members were supplied by the Butterley Company from their Derbyshire Works. Following the opening of this new viaduct the original structure was closed for repairs, which took until April the following year.

As the line of railway approaches the twin viaducts, extensive workings of The Miller's Dale Lime Company are to the left and in former times these provided the Midland with a considerable amount of traffic.

Miller's Dale, so named from the ancient corn mill still used for that purpose and deriving some of its power from the flow of the River Wye, had its station built on a convenient table of land on the hillside 'tailored' by the Midland to accept the original main line and two platforms with the addition, in 1905, of an island bay platform used by trains to and from Buxton. At the same time the single-faced platform alongside the 'down' main line was changed into an island platform so giving four main-line tracks through the station.

During the battle to obtain Parliamentary approval for the line, one of the arguments concerned the requirements of those persons,

particularly any with complaints such as gout, wishing to visit the Spa town of Buxton to take the waters, having to cross the platform from a main-line train in order to reach the branch train. Eventually, this was to some extent solved by the provision of through carriages which were detached from the main-line train and added to that for the branch without the need to disturb occupants. Four such services were running daily in 1903, in addition to branch-line trains which ran in connection with other main-line trains, of which there were seventeen daily. At the turn of the century London was 2¾ hours away by the best train, with Manchester less than an hour's journey, the trip along the branch to Buxton taking a mere 10 minutes.

For such a rural location Miller's Dale station was quite large and boasted a subway connecting 'up', 'down' and branch platforms, whilst

the stone buildings were, to use a Victorian term, 'commodious', providing full passenger facilities. The original buildings were alongside the 'up' line and the single 'down' line platform had a curtain wall. With the 1903-5 alterations an additional station building was provided on the main island platform and a new canopy added for the platform face, whilst waiting room facilities were provided on the new canopied island branch platform.

It was originally intended that its name should be 'Blackwell Mill', this being the nearest village of any size but the name of the hamlet nestling on the banks of the Wye was preferred, with the addition 'For Tideswell' to indicate its proximity to the important small market town some two miles distant.

Pronounced 'Tidsor', this charming and extensive town has a fine fourteenth-century church dedicated to St John the Baptist, containing many items of great beauty, including ten choir stalls with misericords almost 600 years old, an elaborate tomb dated 1358 in memory of John Foljambe, whose family helped to establish Tideswell from the time of the Conquest, and a memorial brass to Robert Pursglove who founded Tideswell Grammar School. In the churchyard is the grave of William Newton, mentioned earlier, and a memorial tablet to Samuel Slack, a chorister with a booming base voice who died in 1822, aged sixty-five, after a life in which he rose to fame by once singing for his King, but who never lost his 'uncouth and earthy demeanour'. After the performance one of the Lords-in-Waiting told Slack how pleased His Majesty had been with his singing to which Slack responded: 'Oh, he wer pleased wor he? Ah, I know'd I could dow't.'

After performances Slack would never associate with other singers but would seek out his own class in some low pot-house and enjoy his clay pipe with a jar of ale. Once, on his way

Top
Class 4F 0-6-0 44470 blasts away from Chee Tor tunnels with a 'down' Easter Monday excursion, 2 April 1956. The signal on the extreme right is for the Buxton branch.

Bottom
The rugged grandeur of the Midland's line through the Peak is encapsulated in this superb shot of ex-Midland 'Compound' 1024 on a 'down' express passing Miller's Dale Junction in 1932.

home and somewhat the worse for drink, he lay down in a field to recover only to awake to find a bull breathing down on him and trying to turn him over with its horns. Slack let out such a bellow with his stentorian bass voice that the bull turned tail and fled! The Chesterfield singers, who had caused his memorial to be raised, acknowledged 'the vacuum in the chorus department occasioned by his loss'.

Tideswell is noted for its Wakes Week, which each year begins on the Saturday nearest to 24 June and includes well dressing and Morris dancing. The present population is around 1,700 and has remained approximately the same down the years. Being more than two miles from the line, the arrival of the railway had a less-marked effect on the town's normal business. Certainly in the days before public road transport took over, the train offered easy access for walkers and hikers to visit this remote spot lying in the middle of the high limestone uplands.

Leaving Miller's Dale station which closed, except for private sidings, to goods traffic on 27 August 1966 and for passengers on 6 March 1967, the line passed the private sidings of the Buxton Lime Firms, originally belonging to the Little Ormes Head Lime Firm and the East Buxton Lime Company, and crossed over the Wye on a viaduct before entering Chee Tor tunnel No. 1 (401 yards), emerged to cross the river again before entering Chee Tor tunnel No. 2 (94 yards). It then emerged for only some 400 yards to run along a ledge carved out of the hillside before entering Rusher Cutting tunnel (121 yards) – which before 1894 had been named Chee Tor No. 3 – then recrossing the Wye on yet another viaduct.

The section of line along this ledge was difficult and expensive to constuct, the cause being the narrow valley through which the Wye passes, its width being too narrow to accept a double-track railway. Chee Tor, a

Top
A 'down' freight train headed by a class 4F 0-6-0 passes an 'up' freight at Blackwell Mill in 1932. The Buxton branch is in the foreground.

Centre
The 'up' platform of the Midland's smallest 'station', Blackwell Mill halt, 9 November 1926. It provided a limited service for railwaymen and their families.

Bottom
Midland 2-4-0 142 heads a train for Buxton along Ashwood Dale in June 1912.

magnificent limestone cliff, towers some 300 feet above the valley bottom and this natural obstacle caused the Midland some headaches during the surveying and construction of the line.

The point at which the present Buxton branch diverges from the main line is Miller's Dale Junction (160 miles and 44 chains from St Pancras), whilst joining the main and branch lines together again a little further to the north is a short length of line which forms the top-side of a triangle linking Peak Forest Junction on the main line with Buxton Junction on the branch. By this means passenger, freight and mineral traffic was able to gain direct access to the Buxton line from the north.

Since closure of the through route to the south of Peak Forest Junction, the section of line between Buxton and Chinley North Junction formerly 'down' has become 'up'.

A traveller between Miller's Dale Junction and Buxton Junction may have glimpsed a small station comprising a pair of offset stone-faced platforms, each equal to the length of just one passenger coach, with a whitewashed stable-like structure set at track level providing limited shelter alongside the 'up' platform's southern end. This was Blackwell Halt, smallest station on the Midland and featured in no timetables, it being a 'staff only' halt where trains stopped, on Fridays and Saturdays, for the benefit of railwaymen who maintained that section and lived nearby with their families. It was variously referred to as 'Blackwell Junction', 'Blackwell Mill' and 'Blackwell Halt' and was in use until 12 June 1966.

Passing Buxton Junction, where the northern leg of the triangle joined from the right, the line entered Wye Dale, following the river and main A6 road into Buxton which held to its southern bank with the railway intertwining and crossing both road and river at high level, in one case by means of an elegant twin-arched

Top
Kirtley 0-6-0 2777 crossing the Wye and the road below Topley Pike on its way to Buxton with a freight train, 30 August 1912.

Centre
The approaches to Buxton Midland station with the excursion platform on the right and the LNWR viaduct in the distance.

Bottom
Midland 2-4-0 1524 at Buxton c1900 awaiting departure with a local train.

girder bridge with a central stone pier. It continued along the dale until it plunged into Pic Tor tunnel (191 yards), referred to as 'Pig Tor' by Midland men, before emerging into picturesque Ashwood Dale where it ran along a ledge hewn from the limestone cliffs lining the valley.

The Ashwood Dale Lime and Buxton Lime Companies' sidings once provided train loads of stone from their quarries and such traffic has been almost the sole reason for the continued use of the Midland branch between Peak Forest Junction and Buxton since passenger traffic ceased in 1967. Buxton Sewage Works interposes between railway and river as the line approaches the outskirts of this famous Spa town, passing through Ashwood Dale tunnel (100 yards) before very soon crossing the borough boundary.

Lying in a protective hollow at the extreme edge of the Pennines but at an altitude of 1,000 feet above sea level Buxton, the highest market town in England, was known to the Romans for the health-giving properties of its waters and they named it 'Aquae Arnementiae'. Much of Buxton's present architectural elegance is owed to its wealthy patrons, particularly the Dukes of Devonshire, and we have to thank the fifth Duke for the supreme beauty of The Crescent, designed by John Carr of York, and completed in 1784 at a cost of £120,000. Other features of the town are the Thermal Baths, by Sir Joseph Paxton; the Pump Room; St Anne's Well; the Devonshire Hospital, also by Carr, with its huge dome 150 feet in diameter and once the largest in the world; the Opera House, which fell from grace to become a cinema but has recently been restored to its former use and glory; Solomon's Temple, a folly tower of 1896 which stands at the top of Grin Low Hill; and the Pavilion Gardens, opened in 1871 and containing twenty-three acres of gardens, with lakes, flower beds, shaded walks and an outdoor games area.

Top
Period street scene in Buxton on 15 June 1897 with the Quadrant in the distance. Note the horse bus and the hackney carriages awaiting hire on the left.

Centre
Taking the waters at St Ann's Well, Buxton, *c*1910.

Bottom
Tobogganing or sledging in the streets at Buxton was clearly a popular sport in 1906.

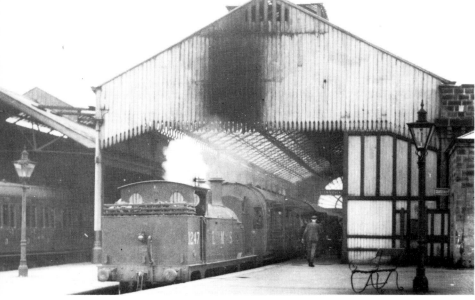

It was to this attractive and popular watering-place that the Midland brought its services on the opening day, Monday 1 June 1863 and for the next four years a through service operated from Derby prior to completion of the extension from Miller's Dale Junction to Manchester in 1867. As explained earlier, from the latter date through carriages were provided on trains to and from London and the town received a steady influx of wealthy and/or chronically sick to test the water's alleged curative powers.

The Midland's line approached the town on a sharp curve and entered its station which, whilst at the top of a hill, was centrally placed. It had two platforms providing three faces (with the later addition of an excursion platform sited just prior to the terminal station) and there was a glass canopied roof with an elegantly arched and glazed end-wall, later to be copied by the London & North Western Railway whose own station was contiguous with and parallel to the Midland's. In 1864 services to and from Derby consisted of six trains daily, of which two were provided to and from London Euston. Only two trains ran in each direction on Sundays between Buxton and Derby.

With the opening of the north curve to Peak Forest Junction a service was instituted from 1 February 1867 to the Manchester terminus of the LNWR at London Road. Through carriages for Liverpool Brunswick had to re-trace their route to Woodley Junction before passing onto the CLC lines. This twenty-mile detour continued until 2 August 1880 when the Cheshire Lines Committee station at Manchester Central was available for use by the Midland.

By 1903 Buxton not only had through services to Manchester in a best time of 48 minutes, but also a through service to Liverpool Central, via Warrington, which took only one hour 51 minutes.

As Buxton Midland the station closed to passengers from 6 March 1967.

The Midland had continued to pursue their objective of reaching Manchester but the LNWR had declined the first Midland proposal which was to jointly continue northwards from Rowsley on the line of the original MBM&MJR route to Manchester on the grounds that the railway would be too costly and had

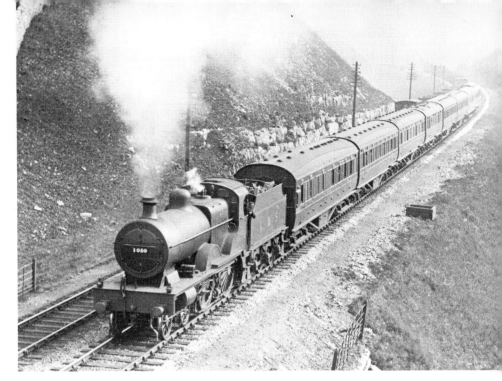

then proceeded to build their own new 'inferior quality' (according to Alport, the Midland's General Manager) line from Whaley Bridge to Buxton which was considered unsuitable for use as a main-line route by the Midland, Alport commenting that it had gone up a steep gradient out of Buxton merely for the sake of going down again and passed through high country areas with little population. However, it unfortunately effectively blocked the way for a new Midland route beyond Buxton.

Alternative routes to Manchester via Stockport and via Hyde were blocked by the LNWR and the MS&LR respectively, acting together with the GNR in a tripartite agreement not approved by Parliament, and the use of a more northerly circuitous route, entering Manchester over the L&YR, was frustrated by yet another tripartite agreement of 1850.

Examining the countryside to find a new and direct through route James Alport, in company with Samuel Beale, the Midland Chairman, and his deputy William Hutchinson, had a chance meeting with an MS&L director and two officials which eventually, after a day spent together, resulted in the latter party suggesting that a new route alongside their own was 'undesirable' and indicating that it might be possible for the Midland to use the MS&L route from New Mills to Manchester. Alport, who had worked for the MS&L for four years and therefore had an intimate

Opposite top
Exterior of Buxton Midland, with the inevitable advertisements *c*1946. The adjacent LNW station was rebuilt in the same style.

Opposite centre
Interesting interior shot of Buxton Midland in LMS days with the usual advertisements, weighing machine, bookstall, and other impedimenta *c*1946.

Opposite bottom
Ex-Midland 0-4-4 tank 1247 at Buxton Midland with a branch passenger train.

Top
LMS 'Compound' 4-4-0 1059 heads through Great Rocks Dale with an express for Manchester Central *c*1934 whilst an 'up' freight passes going south.

Centre
'Stanier' 2-8-0 48741 of Buxton shed on an 'up' freight passing Great Rocks Junction, 28 June 1952.

Bottom
Limestone trains in the ICI sidings at Tunstead, 16 August 1957.

knowledge of their affairs, duly met the MS&L chairman and, despite pressure from the other companies, an agreement was made that the Midland should run its trains over the railways of the MS&L 'to or from Manchester and every other place in Manchester, in Lancashire or Cheshire or beyond'.

The problem of access to Manchester was therefore solved and the Act for making the new Midland line to New Mills, to link up with the MS&L, received Royal Assent in June 1862.

Continuing northwards, the new main line formed one side of the triangle between Miller's Dale Junction (160 miles 44 chains) and Peak Forest Junction, 41 chains further and amidst scenery of great beauty, through Peak Forest Junction tunnel (29 yards) and the 161-yard Great Rocks tunnel, then along Great Rocks Dale, with the large ICI quarry on the left of the line at Tunstead extending for more than two miles into Peak Dale. Extensive quarry sidings were sited here along the lefthand side of the line whilst between Great Rocks Junction and Peak Forest a 'down' goods line was formerly on the left of the main lines.

Peak Forest station (163 miles 66 chains) was built near the summit of the line at 982 feet above sea level. It is a patent misnomer for the nearest village is Small Dale, the village of Peak Forest being almost three miles away! After 1893 the station name-board proclaimed 'Peak Forest for Peak Dale'. There were two platforms either side of the twin-track main line, and the stoutly constructed stone station-house still stands by the remains of the 'down' platform. Accommodation on the 'up' line was a slate-roofed open shelter inside a stone curtain wall, all now demolished.

In later years it was overshadowed by the Buxton Lime Firm's extensive

Top
'Peak Forest for Peak Dale' station, looking north, 24 June 1933. Beyond the road bridge there is the Buxton Lime Firm's plant, erected in 1912.

Centre
A later view of Peak Forest station, 2 August 1960, as 0-6-0 'banker' 43950 sits in the bay awaiting a call to duty and 2-8-0 48605 passed through on an 'up' mineral empties train.

Bottom
'Royal Scot' Class 4-6-0 46162 *Queen's Westminster Rifleman* passes Tunstead with *The Palatine* 'up' express, on 9 July 1960.

operations in the quarry situated just beyond the road overbridge to the north of the station. After taking over the separate firms of Wainwright and Beswick, operations expanded and in 1918 a large stone-plant building was erected which dwarfed the Midland premises below. The sidings actually passed behind the 'up' platform and made a connection with other sidings further south, whilst to the north they once fanned out in all directions. The activities of the stone firms cloak the surrounding area with a fine white dust.

The United Alkali Company had works to the south of the station, and to the north the Great Central Railway Company had an interest for it was from here that the Peak Forest Tramway had begun operations as early as 1799 under the aegis of the Peak Forest Canal Company. The tramway was built to link the quarries of the Dove Holes area with the Bugsworth basin of the Peak Forest canal, with waterway links to Ashton Junction, Marple and Whaley Bridge. The 4 feet 2½ inch gauge tramway, built to Benjamin Outram's standards, used an inclined plane for gravity descent of loaded wagons with horses on the level sections. It was taken over by the Manchester, Sheffield & Lincolnshire Railway in 1863, passed to the Great Central Railway on 1 August 1897 and closed completely in 1926.

Peak Forest village lies on the A623 road, some five miles from Buxton and has been described as Derbyshire's 'Gretna Green' as the resident church minister, by virtue of an ancient office, was able to record 'foreign marriages' without the need for parental permission, license, witness or any other obstacle! This was banned by Act of Parliament in July 1804. The original church, dedicated to 'St Charles Kinge and Martyr' was erected in 1657 but was replaced by

Top
A 'Belpaire' 4-4-0 and a Johnson 4-2-2 combine forces to double-head an express near Peak Forest around the beginning of this century.

Centre
The challenge of the Peak Forest area is seen clearly in this shot of 0-6-0 44262 in the deep rock cutting at the approaches to Peak Forest with an 'up' goods, 30 March 1957.

Bottom
'Compound' 4-4-0 1016 emerges from Dove Holes tunnel with an express, 2 August 1926.

the present one, a gift of the Duke of Devonshire, in 1878. Peak Forest is a 'dry' village for there is no public house, though at Peak Dale the Midland Hotel supplies local needs and once boasted a sign featuring the Midland Railway's 4-4-0 Compound express locomotive No. 1000 since changed for a humble 0-6-0.

Except for private sidings the station closed to goods traffic on 15 June 1964 and to passengers from 6 March 1967.

Leaving Peak Forest, a branch on the right at Peak Forest North leads to Taylor, Frith & Company's sidings and connects with the Dove Holes quarries and then, having reached the summit of the line nearly 1,000 feet above sea level and 164 miles 7 chains from London, the railway enters the southern end of the 2,984-yard Dove Holes tunnel, longest on the route, and passing 183 feet beneath the L&NWR Buxton branch on its way across the moor below Black Edge, eventually emerged to pass under that line as the LNWR swings towards Whaley Bridge and Stockport, before entering Chapel-en-le-Frith station.

Dove Holes tunnel was a mammoth engineering task and although the lowest tender price was £175,565, its estimated cost on completion was only £135,986. It drops 99½ feet between the southern and northern portals, the line being on a constant 1 in 90 gradient, the best that, as Mr Barlow observed 'could be obtained without going underground altogether'. Cut through solid rock below Cow Low, the Midland Railway themselves built the tunnel, Mr Barlow appointing James Campbell to carry out the work. A river was encountered and diverted during construction work, only to re-appear later in the excavations. The second diversion resulted in a partial drying-up of the well-known Barmoor Clough 'Ebbing and Flowing Well' which, in earlier times, had been considered one of the wonders of the Peak. It now rarely

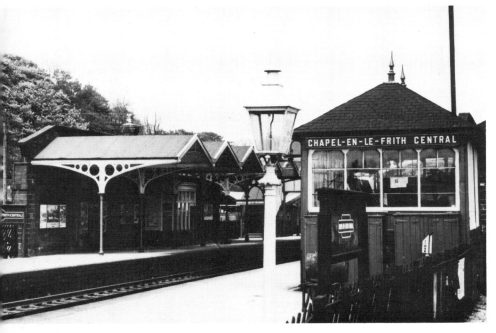

Top
Chapel-en-le-Frith Central station looking north, 9 July 1967.

Centre
Chapel-en-le-Frith Central station looking south, showing Midland awning, signal box and gas lamp, 2 June 1955.

Bottom
Market Street, Chapel-en-le-Frith, in the early 1930s.

functions but during periods of really heavy rain may flow for a few minutes in any one hour. Six pumping engines, varying in size from 20 to 50hp were employed in clearing the tunnel of water from many springs exposed during the work.

Navvies lived in mud-daubed or rough stone huts, or in rock recesses and had to extemporise facilities to the best of their ability. There were inevitable disagreements and at one point Irish navvies were driven off the working area by the English and returned only after the engineer provided police protection.

Being cut through limestone for one-third of its length and the remainder through sandstone and shale, the tunnel still needed regular attention and in fact it collapsed in June 1872 when only five years old, and again after torrential rain in February 1940. On the latter occasion a southbound goods train ran into a rock fall but a second train, travelling in the opposite direction, was saved by the quick-thinking actions of the guard of the first train.

Leaving Dove Holes tunnel the line emerges on a table-land which forms a watershed between Black Brook to the east and the brooks flowing westward towards Whaley Bridge. It traverses this table of land and runs into Chapel-en-le-Frith station (167 miles 42 chains) which first opened for goods traffic on 1 October 1866 and for passengers on 1 February 1867. The name was changed to Chapel-en-le-Frith Central on 2 June 1924 to distinguish it from Chapel-en-le-Frith South on the nearby ex-LNWR section of the LMS.

The Midland station had its main buildings on the 'up' platform to a design almost identical to those at Rowsley and Bakewell. A goods loop avoided the station to pass behind the

Top
The essence of the Midland – an 'up' express at Chapel-en-le-Frith *c*1904 headed by a '1312' Class 4-4-0 passing a veteran lengthsman, complete with crowbar and keying hammer, as he checks his section of track for loose keys or any other defects.

Centre
An 'up' express enters Chapel-en-le-Frith with an '1808' class 4-4-0 piloting a '2421' series 4-4-0, just after the turn of the century.

Bottom
Fine action shot of ex-Midland 'Compound' 4-4-0 1020 at the head of an 'up' express near Chapel-en-le-Frith *c*1933.

Chapel Milton
(showing Eccles Pike)
119.

'down' platform and rejoin the main line at Chinley South Junction.

Chapel-en-le-Frith is an old market town with a fourteenth-century church dedicated to St Thomas of Canterbury, built on the site of a former chapel founded in 1226 by the local foresters and keepers of the Royal Forest, hence its name 'The Chapel in the Frith' (or Forest). The church is now known as Derbyshire's 'Black Hole', for in the year 1648 a Scottish army of fifteen hundred men, after defeat at Preston whilst supporting Charles I under the Duke of Hamilton, was marched here and incarcerated in the church for sixteen days, despite its lack of air and space. Before their release forty had died, with another ten en route to Cheshire, and they are buried in the churchyard, a sad testament to 'man's inhumanity to man'.

Modern industry, of course, has invaded this small town but some of its former charms remain including much of the old market place, complete with stocks. A 'pudding bell' is still rung an hour early at eleven o'clock on Shrove Tuesday morning to remind housewives to mix their pancake batter in good time. A 'curfew bell' has been rung since the year 1070, and two Sunday bells are still rung at eight o'clock in the morning and one o'clock in the afternoon.

Nearby Tunstead is noted for its ancient human skull, with its name of 'Dicky of Tunstead', which has been preserved in a farmhouse for generations and is said to have supernatural powers. Those who have attempted either to move or get rid of it have, so the legend says, suffered dire consequences, and today it remains in its favoured place.

Leaving Chapel-en-le-Frith the railway crosses both the Black Brook and

Top
The 4.25pm express from Manchester Central passing Chinley South Junction, 19 June 1957, with 'Jubilee' class 4-6-0 45598 *Basutoland* in charge.

Centre
Chapel Milton viaduct which splits into two, with the nearer section leading to the Dore line and a down train on the Manchester line part of the viaduct furthest from the camera – view taken about 1912.

Bottom
Class 4F 0-6-0 44380 on an 'up' Derby stopping train at Chinley North Junction, 3 September 1955. The line to Derby is to the right and the Dore line curves to the left.

the route of the former Peak Forest Tramway, on its way through Chapel Milton, by means of a stone viaduct of fifteen arches around 100 feet in height. Chinley South Junction was sited on this viaduct to carry a line directly connecting with the Dore and Chinley line, at Chinley East Junction, a distance of 31 chains, and the viaduct splits into two to make this possible. The north curve between Chinley East and North Junctions completes the triangle.

Continuing via Chinley North, where crossover roads formerly provided for separation into both fast and slow double-track main lines by means of the alterations carried out in 1902-3, the railway now runs into the remains of the once large station at Chinley.

The first Chinley station, opened with the original through route on 1 February 1867, was a modest affair located further east of the present site and closed on 1 June 1902 when the new and larger station opened six chains further west. The building of the new station, which stands some 680 feet above sea level, was made necessary by the construction of the New Mills and Heaton Mersey railway which by-passed both Stockport and Marple, thus requiring a new point of junction between trains to Manchester Central, Manchester Victoria and Liverpool. The new station also provided a convenient terminus for Dore and Chinley line local trains which hitherto had run to Buxton.

The first and original station comprised a fine twin-tabled stone-built station house which also accommodated various elements of a typical country station of the period, and was the focal point of local activities. On its closure the station house was carefully taken down, stone by stone, and re-erected as a detached residence on Maynestone Road on the

edge of the village.

Upon the construction of the large new station, with its five through and one bay platforms, Chinley's importance increased from a mere wayside country station to a major junction, and Midland services were much improved with many trains being divided and re-marshalled, and it was the point from which trains to Manchester were provided in both express and stopping categories. Trains from Derby and the south, from the Buxton branch, and from Sheffield via the Hope valley line, converged here, whilst to the north destinations included both Central and Victoria stations in Manchester, Liverpool and Blackpool. In 1903, the best time to Central was 26 minutes and to Liverpool Central 71 minutes. The station today is but a shadow of its former self, a solitary island platform serving today's passengers.

Chinley's goods yard continued in use until 7 October 1963.

Chinley village, overlooked by Chinley Churn (cairn), 1,484 feet high, is a scattered settlement and with Bugsworth and Brownside forms a joint township in the Hayfield Chapelry. Industries have included paper and cotton wool manufactories and a colliery, but it is probably more known for its associations with the Reverend William Bagshaw, the 'Apostle of the Peak', who was ejected from the vicarage after sixteen years in consequence of the passing of the Act of Uniformity of 1662, but who continued his great work from Ford Hall nearby. Population of the area at the turn of the century, having remained dormant for most of the previous century, was around 1,200.

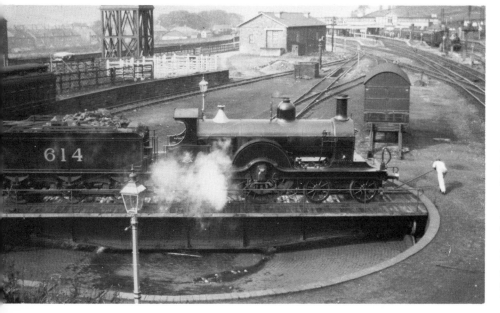

Top
Midland 4-4-0 504, fitted for oil burning, stands at Chinley, with an express for St Pancras, 27 July 1921.

Centre
A Midland 4-4-0, possible 344, on a 'down' express at Chinley *c*1920.

Bottom
'Johnson Single' 614 from Liverpool is turned by hand on Chinley turntable with the station in the background, 7 August 1923.

6
Routes to Manchester

Part I – Routes to Manchester London Road:

As described in the previous chapter, a variety of railway routes opened up for the traveller on the Midland north of Chinley but for the first few miles a single route contained northbound traffic.

Leaving Chinley the line follows the sweep of the valley until it reaches Bugsworth, location of the most serious problem encountered on this section for scarcely had goods traffic commenced to New Mills on 1 October 1866 than the whole of the area was swamped by a persistent deluge, as a result of which sixteen acres of land north of Bugsworth station slipped towards the valley, taking the Midland viaduct with it. Of necessity, trains were suspended and for a period of ten weeks over four hundred men were employed night and day, 'as many as could find elbow room to work', in an effort to divert the line to solid ground when the bottom of the landslip was drained with the construction of underground headings of some depth, with lateral channels in all directions.

A new viaduct was constructed using 50,000 feet of Baltic timber, two 30-foot-span skew bridges of wrought iron girders were erected and a deep rock-cutting excavated at one end, with a connecting embankment made of 25,000 tons of ash and 32,000 tons of earth, stone and clay, at the other end to complete the work.

The timber viaduct was a temporary solution but served until 1885 when the present embankment, built between the slipped and the timber viaducts, was brought into use. Its

Previous page
Midland 'Compound' 1018 makes a spectacular start from Manchester Central with a southbound express in the summer of 1911. This Midland official photograph was considered to be so good that the LMS used it after 1923 carefully having the letters 'MR' blacked out on the locomotive's buffer beam!

Top
'Up' express from Manchester passing Bugsworth headed by 4-4-0 447 *c*1920.

Centre
Bugsworth station 'down' platform, looking towards Derby.

Bottom
Buxworth station buildings, 21 November 1970, looking towards Chinley. The original intended alignment of the railway passed on the opposite side of the station buildings causing them to change from being on the 'up' to the 'down' side!

design and construction were supervised by Mr A. A. Langley and finally the old viaduct, except for the first bridge at the southern end, was blown up with the use of gunpowder.

During this blockage, traffic was diverted via Eckington (Derbyshire) and the MS&L line over Woodhead but goods traffic resumed on 24 January 1867 with passenger services on 1 February, three months later than planned, thereby instituting the first Midland through service between London King's Cross and Manchester. (St Pancras station was not, of course, opened for use until 1 October 1868.)

With the widening of the route to four tracks in 1902–3 Bugsworth tunnel, on the Manchester side of the station, was opened out to become a deep cutting. When this tunnel was originally being excavated its mouth caved in, trapping a gang of navvies. 'Well chaps', said one to the rest, 'we shall never get out alive so we may as well go on with our bit, while we can.' They worked on hacking at the rock face in the flickering candlelight until one by one they fell limp and dying in the heavy oxygen-drained air. Rescuers reached them just as their candles were guttering.

Bugsworth station (170 miles 35 chains) was renamed 'Buxworth' from 4 June 1930 after residents petitioned for the name to be changed owing to its obvious connotations. It was closed on 15 September 1958 although the buildings still remain. Buxworth (Bugsworth) is a small place with one main street and nowadays has only a few small businesses and factories. It is the terminus of a branch of the Peak Forest canal leading to Whaley Bridge, where the former Cromford and High Peak Railway had its terminus. In the last century Bugsworth was described as a 'thriving inland canal port' and had canal basins capable of holding twenty or so longboats, with loading sheds and stabling for forty horses. Canal and Peak

Top
45561 *Saskatchewan*, a 'Jubilee' from Bristol shed, passing Buxworth in 1952 with a Manchester Central to Derby stopping train.

Centre
'Compound' 4-4-0 1063 leaving New Mills tunnel and passing over Sett viaduct at the head of an 'up' stopping train.

Bottom
New Mills Junction looking east, with the Great Central and Midland branch to Hayfield on the left, and the Midland line to Chinley on the right.

Forest Tramway traffic brought a certain prosperity to the township which consequently expanded with mills, quarries and coalmines all being developed from the various wharves, and the place hummed with enterprise.

Today the tramway is no more, the station is closed and Buxworth relies on road facilities for its trade and transport, though the canal basin again thrives as a narrow-boat centre for pleasure and some commercial traffic.

From Buxworth the line passes the site of Buxworth Junction and reaches the site of Gowhole sorting sidings, where the 'down' yard was between the present running lines and the site of the former slow lines, with the 'up' yard on the far side of the latter before New Mills South Junction, where routes diverge. Gowhole sidings marked the convergence of a number of routes from the north and west at a point where definable train loads for the south and east could be made up.

Leaving New Mills South Junction the line passes New Mills Goods station (which closed on 9 September 1968), passes over Sett Viaduct high above the often-torrent-like Sett river, through the 120-yard New Mills tunnel and then joins the branch from Hayfield which emerges from a separate tunnel on the right at New Mills Junction. Here, on what became joint Manchester, Sheffield & Lincolnshire and Midland metals in the form of the 'Sheffield and Midland Committee', the railway enters New Mills station (173 miles 15 chains).

The 2⅞-mile branch to Hayfield which commenced, so far as the Midland was concerned, at New Mills Junction was constructed by Rennie and Company at a cost of £27,040 to double track standards although a single line only was laid, except for the first 28 chains through the 197-yard Hayfield tunnel. An intermediate single-platform station was provided at Birch Vale (opened May 1868) along with a small goods yard, and the single platform at the Hayfield terminus had a run-round loop and extensive sidings. Construction of this branch was part of the separate Marple, New Mills and Hayfield Junction Railway, a promotion of the MS&LR Company, who had powers to lease and work it after construction. It was built to link their existing branch from the main line at Hyde Junction to Marple with Hayfield, an

important manufacturing centre in the highest section of the Peak, where the attraction of water power from the swirling waters of the River Sett, initiated cotton, paper and calico printing mills at Park Hall.

In the churchyard is a gravestone to Martha Cundy who died in 1759, aged 41, but by a mason's error the stone originally had a 'nought' between the 'four' and the 'one'. After a wag wrote a two-line comment:

Martha Cundy is dead and gone
Her age is just four hundred and one

the mason took his mallet and chisel and erased the offending 'zero'.

Passenger services on the Hayfield branch began on 1 March 1868 and regular goods traffic on 18 March 1872, coal traffic having commenced on 7 April 1870. The entire line from Hayfield through New Mills to Hyde was taken over by the new 'Sheffield & Midland Committee', a joint vesting body of the MS&L and Midland companies (incorporated on 1 January 1870 in accordance with an Act of Parliament dated 24 June 1869).

At the point where the two lines from Hayfield and Chinley emerge from their separate tunnels to meet at New Mills Junction, passengers little appreciate the engineering work necessary to secure a foothold for the junction. It sits on a rocky shelf literally blasted out of the hillside, with a huge supporting wall to the right, and to the left a massive retaining wall with its base in the waters of the River Goyt as it swirls along the rocky channel some 40 feet below.

New Mills station had been opened for traffic on 1 July 1865 as

Opposite top
Hayfield station, 24 July 1949.

Opposite centre
Church Street, Hayfield, *c*1904 is the subject of this Victorian scene.

Opposite bottom
New Mills Central looking east, 29 October 1984, with the 'down' platform and stationmaster's house on the right. New Mills Junction signal box is just beyond the foot and road overbridges.

Top
New Mills Central looking towards Strines, 29 October 1984.

Centre
Market Street, New Mills, *c*1906. 'Prize Dairy Butter' is on sale in the grocers on the right at one shilling (5p) per pound!

Bottom
Strines station looking towards New Mills in Midland days.

part of the above-mentioned scheme and was thus ready to receive the first Midland through passenger train when the section of line from Miller's Dale opened in February 1867. The stone station buildings on the 'down' (Manchester) platform are still intact and at the north end, also on the platform, stands the elegant stone-built stationmaster's house with the top gable dated 1864. The station sits in a niche in the hillside with steep slopes above and below.

Today, as New Mills Central, it is still a busy place and marks the termination of the diesel multiple unit suburban service from Manchester Piccadilly which utilises the Hayfield tunnel for stabling purposes, the branch having closed on 5 January 1970, goods services ceasing on 15 April 1963 at Hayfield and on 2 November 1964 at Birch Vale. There are some twenty-five stopping and eight fast trains to Manchester daily, compared to fourteen MS&L and a mere three Midland trains in 1887.

The next station beyond New Mills is Strines (174 miles 48 chains), completed in the summer of 1866, following the earlier opening of a section between New Mills and Marple for passengers on 1 July 1865. Strines station is approached by means of a winding road and is some distance from its village, which straggles along the Goyt valley alongside the B6101 road, sandwiched between the railway on the east side, with Mellor Moor rising beyond, and the Peak Forest canal to the west.

The original MS&L station buildings comprised a stone-built booking office and waiting-room with a two-storey stationmaster's house, also in stone, on the south side. A large goods shed stood in the 'down' side goods yard at the south end and a wrought-iron footbridge was provided over the tracks to the 'up' platform, where accommodation consisted of a hipped slate-roofed timber-boarded waiting-room with an open-arched front. The station signal box was situated at the

Top
The 'down' side station buildings at Strines in the 1960s, before demolition.

Centre
Marple station looking north as it once was. All was swept away apart from the footbridge in the modernisation, completed in 1970.

Bottom
'Compound' 4-4-0 1089 stands at Marple with an 'up' stopping train, 21 April 1935.

south end of the 'up' platform and controlled traffic through the station and into the goods yard on the opposite side of the main line.

An unstaffed halt from 10 September 1973, the station today presents a sad aspect, for all facilities, including the goods yard and signal box, have been swept away and each platform now boasts a single crude stone-built shelter with a sloping concrete roof. Twenty-four stopping trains daily call for Manchester with twenty-five in the opposite direction. Saturday services are eighteen and seventeen respectively, with eight and ten on Sundays.

The railway at this point follows the meanderings of the River Goyt as it threads its way through the valley and in a further two miles or so, having crossed the river which marked the old county boundary between Derbyshire and Cheshire by means of Viaduct No. 23 and passing through the 225-yard Marple South tunnel, reaches Marple station (176 miles 57 chains).

From April 1875, when the curve at Romiley was opened, Marple was for many years an important interchange point on the Midland route for it was here that some carriages for Liverpool were detached for forward working, or combined with southbound trains from Manchester. By using Marple as a detaching point the Midland, in the first year, saved themselves many miles of unproductive working, and the arrangement continued until 2 August 1880 when Manchester Central station was adopted as the new Midland terminus and trains worked through via the curve at Romiley to Stockport Tiviot Dale (Cheshire Lines) station and thence via Heaton Mersey and Chorlton-cum-Hardy, after which Marple's importance was lessened for a time.

By way of brief explanation the original Cheshire Lines group had been formed by the Great Northern and Manchester, Sheffield & Lincolnshire railway companies which joined forces under the Great Northern (Cheshire Lines) Act of Parliament dated 13 July 1863 to operate hitherto independent authorised lines in Cheshire, pre-dated by the establishment of a joint GN and

MS&L Committee on 11 June 1862 to regulate traffic on four railways already authorised but not by then open. The Midland became an equal partner on 18 July 1866 to what by then had become the 'Cheshire Lines Committee' by means of the Cheshire Lines Transfer Act of 5 July 1865, having a management group of three directors from each of the companies. 'The Cheshire Lines Act' of 15 August 1867 authorised the railway as a fully independent concern with its own seal, retained under the joint control of the three companies.

Marple stands on the River Goyt and is served by the Peak Forest and Macclesfield canals and is quite an important trading centre for the region, cotton once being a staple trade. At the turn of the century it had a population of some 5,500.

Marple station had been brought into use on 5 August 1862 as part of the extension of the Hyde Branch of the MS&L. In its heyday it was busy serving both the MS&L and Midland companies. On the Manchester platforms there were extensive station buildings at the south end including a stationmaster's house. A bay platform was provided at the north end on the 'down' side, whilst the 'up' side consisted of an island platform approached by a footbridge from the road overbridge at the south end of the station.

Locomotive watering facilities were provided and on the east side there were two turntables, the Midland, about 1897 and at their own expense, having provided a second and larger 50-foot one to the south of the road overbridge when their partners were

Centre
Marple station *c*1910 with a Hayfield branch passenger train headed by Great Central 2-4-2 tank 735.

Bottom
Marple Bridge *c*1920.

unwilling to agree to the scheme, the existing 45-foot one being large enough for the shorter locomotives used on MS&L services. When the Midland ceased detaching carriages at Marple this second turntable was moved, c1913, to Buxton to assist in turning the 4-4-0 locomotives by then in use.

In 1875 some thirty-four 'up' and thirty-two 'down' passenger trains called at Marple. Seven 'up' and six 'down' trains were Midland expresses and all but one attached or detached Liverpool portions. Running non-stop from Derby to Marple, the best trains reached Manchester London Road from St Pancras in 4 hours 45 minutes. A Liverpool portion, conveying a through Pullman drawing-room car, took 65 minutes to reach its destination, calling at Stockport Tiviot Dale and Warrington. Some Manchester trains also conveyed Pullman cars. With the opening of Manchester Central station in 1880 the pattern changed, the Midland in 1884 finally giving up its local services to London Road.

During the year 1970 Marple station was reconstructed. The old loop line and the bay platform on the 'down' side had already been dispensed with by 1966 and only the two main platform faces remained. Two new extensive brick-built waiting rooms were constructed on the Manchester side and a new booking office and hall were built on the other. The MS&L buildings were demolished the same year and the rebuilt station commenced operations on 28 October 1970. All that now remains are the platforms and the old footbridge, numbered 27. The station signal box at the north end on the 'up' platform disappeared with the introduction of colour-light signalling in July 1980.

One of the new waiting rooms has

Top left
Part of Marple aqueduct which carries the Peak Forest canal over the river Goyt.

Top right
Music hath charms – a delightful scene in the garden of Slack Wood Cottage, Mellor, as a venerable gentleman, possibly a mill worker, relaxes by playing the cello.

Centre
Samuel Oldknow's warehouse beside the Peak Forest canal at Marple, part way up the flight of sixteen locks.

Bottom
A multi-view picture postcard of Marple featuring some of its many attractions. Marple is still a delightful place to visit.

already suffered vandalisation and been put out of use whilst the other is spartan and rather unwelcoming; a contrast to Midland waiting rooms of bygone days with their upholstered seats, travel posters and wall pictures, and the cheerful glow of a coal fire in an attractive fireplace to welcome travellers.

Marple Bridge is a small village nestling on the east side of the main road and extends a little way up the hill towards the station along the main road after it crosses the River Goyt. Further up the same hill the old cotton warehouse of Samuel Oldknow makes a pleasing picture as it stands at the side of Peak Forest canal, part-way down a flight of sixteen locks as the canal drops a total of 210 feet from its junction with the Macclesfield Canal at the edge of Marple, on its way to Ashton-under-Lyne. The old warehouse, dating from 1796, suffered years of misuse and neglect but has recently been restored and put to modern use by firms involved in graphic design, architecture and office environment designs.

Marple village has been considerably enlarged over the past century to become a dormitory for Stockport but has managed to retain some of its former charm. But gone are the days when John Bradshaw Isherwood of Marple Hall was patron and known as 'The Squire' and shopkeepers valued his patronage. Authority eventually passed to the mill and factory owners and is now disseminated wider afield. Samuel Oldknow of Stockport, mentioned previously, was one who prospered by his invention of a spinning mule for making strong but fine muslin yarn. He it was who built up the mills at Marple and Mellor. He employed around 400 people in his mill, built a boatyard, a dock and warehouses, and developed the farming of sheep and cattle in the area.

Leaving Marple and passing through the 99-yard Marple North tunnel, the line reaches Marple Wharf

Top
'Compound' 4-4-0 41154 at Marple with the 1.04pm Manchester Central to Sheffield stopping train, 25 May 1953.

Centre
Almost unrecognisable compared to the other photographs – Marple as it is today, seen from the road overbridge looking north, 29 October 1984.

Bottom
Romiley station looking towards Manchester, 21 July 1970.

Junction where the short branch line from Rose Hill, Marple, joins from the left. This former Great Central and North Staffordshire Joint Committee line originally ran through to Macclesfield but was closed to passengers on 5 May 1970 and subsequently lifted. Resuming the journey to Manchester the railway passes over the immense stone-arched viaduct (No. 30), some 308 yards long, which crosses both the Peak Forest canal and the embryo River Mersey, a little distance from its source and formation at the confluence of the Goyt and Etherow rivers on the moors above Marple. (Other modern sources, however, declare that the Mersey begins at Stockport!). Running alongside the viaduct is the Marple aqueduct on the Peak Forest canal, a fine stone structure completed in 1800 which spans the River Goyt in three arches, 100 feet above the waters below.

Romiley station (178 miles 28 chains), which stands on the north side of the B6104 road, is the next on the route, its platforms extending across the wrought-iron lattice girder bridge which carries the railway over that thoroughfare. It had been opened by the MS&L on 5 August 1862 as part of the extension of their Hyde branch as far as Marple.

Still largely intact, with buildings on both platforms, it has a stationmaster's house at the northern end of the extensive buildings on the Manchester platform and is a little unusual in having a spiral staircase, once complete with a fine glass-domed roof but which is now missing. From street level passengers ascend to the first floor where the booking hall and office are sited and a subway with a further flight of stairs affords communication to the platforms.

Romiley today is still a busy station with fifty-seven trains to, and fifty-five from, Manchester of which twenty-six terminate at Marple Rose Hill with two going through to Marple. Ten fewer trains run on Saturdays with nine to, and eleven from, Manchester on Sundays.

Top
The 'up' platform buildings at Romiley looking south, 29 October 1984.

Centre
Romiley station entrance from the street below in 1984.

Bottom
Barlow Fold, Romiley *c*1912 – a picturesque corner of Cheshire.

Immediately beyond Romiley is a three-way junction, controlled by Romiley Junction signal box, the left pair of diverging lines formerly heading to Bredbury Junction followed by a further pair of lines to Bredbury station and beyond, the line continuing until, a little further on, it runs onto the curve bringing it to Woodley (179 miles 46 chains) to link with the old Stockport & Woodley Junction route.

The line to Bredbury Junction was authorised by the Act of 24 June 1869 which brought the Sheffield & Midland Committee into being, this body taking over responsibility for the Hyde Junction to Hayfield line and the stations in between, formerly the sole responsibility of the MS&L.

Top
Romiley looking west, towards the end of the last century as a Midland 4-2-2 approaches with an 'up' express on the line from Bredbury Junction.

Centre
'Jubilee' 4-6-0 45649 *Hawkins* heads an express along the line to Bredbury Junction in 1952 to join the old CLC route.

Bottom
Fine period scene at Woodley station in the early part of this century as passengers await the arrival of a 'down' train.

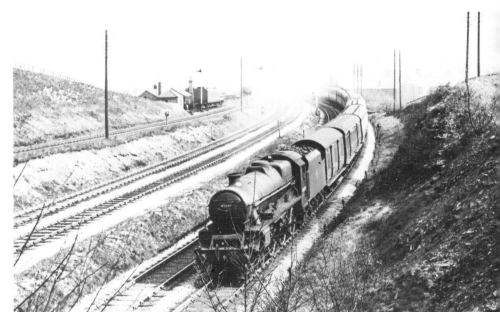

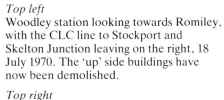

Top left
Woodley station looking towards Romiley, with the CLC line to Stockport and Skelton Junction leaving on the right, 18 July 1970. The 'up' side buildings have now been demolished.

Top right
Company Seal of the Sheffield and Midland Railway Companies Committee, incorporated on 6 August 1872.

Centre
Woodley station exterior, 31 October 1984.

Bottom
Apethorne Junction with its unusual signal box, looking east towards Hyde in early BR days. The now abandoned CLC line to Godley Junction branched off here.

From Woodley, opened 5 August 1862, which has only lost its original accommodation on the 'up' line, along with its extensive goods yard once a hive of activity beside the junction, the line passes via Apethorne Junction (where the now abandoned CLC line to Godley Junction branched off) and then through Hyde (181 miles 8 chains) which was opened at the end of a branch from Newton on the main Sheffield, Ashton-under-Lyne and Manchester line on 1 March 1858.

Hyde, at the end of a high-curving viaduct, was once a busy station with extensive buildings on the New Mills platform and both platforms had large shelters, the south side one being at the east end of the station buildings. These were all demolished about eight years ago with the exception of the Manchester platform shelter, which still remains. A new booking office was provided at street level and a small corrugated-roofed shelter provided on the New Mills platform.

112

From here the line continues along a viaduct, crossing the two main roads and a motorway and enters Hyde Junction station which has platforms only on the S&M line and first appeared in the timetable in February 1863. Via the junction itself the route then runs onto the SA&M (later MS&L then Great Central) main line at 182 miles 11 chains where S&M joint responsibilities ended.

Timed to take place between October 1984 and January 1985 the junction at Hyde was altered and signalling changed, with temporary wooden platforms provided either side of the main electrified line between Manchester Piccadilly and Glossop. The overhead equipment, over thirty years old, is now changed to modern 25kv standards.

Top
Hyde station *c*1950, looking towards Manchester. All the buildings on the 'up' platform have since been demolished.

Centre
The 'down' platform shelter at Hyde Central, 31 October 1984.

Bottom
Market Street Hyde *c*1907.

The original MS&L station buildings on the Manchester-direction platform have been demolished and only the original footbridge remains. Now a small modern booking office and two very basic shelters provide for passengers' needs.

From here the route lay over GCR metals through Guide Bridge (183 miles 39 chains), Fairfield – for Droylsden (184 miles 66 chains), Gorton (185 miles 26 chains) Ashburys (186 miles 28 chains) and Ardwick (187 miles 46 chains) to arrive in London Road station with a total route mileage from St Pancras of 187 miles 74 chains.

Top
Hyde North, formerly the Great Central & Midland Joint Hyde Junction station, looking towards Manchester, 22 May 1971. All the buildings have since been demolished.

Centre
Hyde North Junction looking south, with the line to Glossop on the left, and Hyde North station and the line to Romiley on the right. Taken on 31 October 1984, this view shows the temporary platforms installed whilst the Hyde line was disconnected during the relaying of the junction.

Bottom
Manchester London Road station where Midland trains terminated until transferred to Central station.

Top
The Midland goods yard at Ancoats –
photograph probably taken in May 1922 –
set amidst the streets of the Manchester
suburb.

Centre
A second view of Ancoats on the same
date, this time showing the goods yard and
offices and a variety of horse-drawn carts
and wagons. The enormous Midland grain
warehouse can be seen on the right.

Bottom
Ashburys station looking towards Hyde
Junction along the route taken by Midland
trains to reach London Road.

The Midland began using this route
and the MS&L stations between
Hyde Junction and Manchester from
1 February 1867 and shared the use
of the old SA&M platforms at
London Road, that company having
by then amalgamated with others to
form the Manchester, Sheffield &
Lincolnshire Railway on 1 January
1847. The agreement with the
Midland to use London Road station
was entered into on 7 November
1861 for fourteen years, 'thereafter
subject to three years notice'
calculated from 1 January 1862.

At Ashburys West Junction, just beyond Ashburys station, the Midland branch to its Ancoats goods station, 1 mile 9 chains in length, also made a connection with the Lancashire & Yorkshire Railway system, branching off at Ancoats Junction, 13 chains beyond Ashburys West Junction and joining the L&Y's Ardwick branch at Midland Junction (187 miles 20 chains from St Pancras, via Hyde).

On the Ancoats branch, and 18 chains beyond Ancoats Junction, another pair of lines diverged in a facing direction to serve the Midland's Ashton Road Coal depot, and in a trailing direction, passing beneath the connection to the L&Y and then reversing again, a branch served the Midland's Goods & Cattle depot.

The Ancoats curve (Ancoats Junction to Midland Junction) was constructed under powers granted to the Midland by an Act of 16 July 1885 and running powers had been granted on 26 November 1884 by the L&Y enabling Midland trains to run from Midland Junction to Manchester Victoria and thence through to Hellifield, and also from Liverpool Exchange to Blackburn. From 1 July 1888 the Midland took over the working of Scottish traffic between Liverpool Exchange, Manchester Victoria and Hellifield. The Ancoats curve opened for passenger traffic on 1 July 1889 with through trains from St Pancras to Manchester Victoria, and for the next two decades the Midland worked many of the Manchester and Blackburn trains with through carriages from St Pancras, with an L&Y Second-Class vehicle attached – the Midland having abolished Second-Class on 1 January 1875. This Ancoats curve is still used today as a busy freight line and by the Harwich/Nottingham services to and from Glasgow which now call at Manchester Victoria.

Top
Ashton Road wagon shops, formerly the Midland's goods and cattle depot, as it was on 31 October 1984.

Centre
The Ancoats curve viaduct, with the track beneath feeding the Ashton Road depot which lies to the right behind the photographer.

Bottom
B1 Class 4-6-0 61366 on Midland metals, leaving the Ancoats Junction viaduct with a Hyde and Hadfield half-day excursion to Blackpool to run on to the L&Y line from Ardwick on the extreme right, 16 May 1954.

Top
London Road station at Manchester just before the First World War.

Centre
Midland 4-4-0 384 about to leave Manchester Victoria with an express *c*1910.

Bottom
Midland 4-6-0 383 piloting another engine of the same class passing Manchester Exchange station *c*1910.

London Road Station, Manchester

Midland traffic in the Manchester area rapidly developed with the opening of the through route from the south and the new Ancoats depot, occupying a 70-acre site and costing nearly half-a-million pounds, opened in the spring of 1870, was soon humming with business in the heart of the city, a mere half-mile from London Road station.

The Midland had thus reached the city of cotton and canals, with a history dating back to Roman times, a woollen industry going back to the fourteenth century and the export of cotton goods to 1760. Communication had been greatly improved in 1761 by using the Bridgewater canal, followed by the opening of the Liverpool and Manchester Railway on 1 September 1830, the first of many to whose ranks the Midland had now been added at an important point in the city's rapid industrial growth.

The Manchester Ship Canal, opened in 1894, made the city an important inland port through links with other waterways and the sea. Its great buildings include the million-pound Gothic Town Hall of 1877 designed by Sir Alfred Waterhouse, a Royal Infirmary funded largely by 'Swedish Nightingale' Jenny Lind's concerts, the Corporation Art Gallery designed by Sir Charles Barry, and the Free Trade Hall, home of the famous Hallé Orchestra with which the name of Sir John Barbirolli will always be connected. When Sir Hamilton Harty was its chief conductor he would be approached at the interval and asked what time the performance would finish for, based on his reply, arrangements were made by the various railway companies, including the Midland, to hold their last trains to cater for the concertgoers.

THE "SEVEN STARS", MANCHESTER.

Other notable buildings which must be mentioned are the vast John Rylands' Library – a 'cathedral of literature' and repository of precious manuscripts, founded by his widow in memory of that self-made and wealthy Lancashire man; the Manchester Grammar School with a history dating from the year 1515; and the Whitworth Art Gallery of 1889, dedicated in memory of the founder of engineering standards.

Apart from the cotton trade, now very contracted, engineering, chemical, and a diversity of other modern industries exist on all sides. Manchester claims to be Britain's second-largest city with some 8,500 shops and a population which has risen from 544,000 in 1900 to some 2 million today. It is constantly being improved, modernised and developed in a very real way and its new shopping centres and perimeter housing estates which 'permit city folk formerly condemned to pass part of their lives in dismal surroundings to live full and happy lives', testify to the survival of its enterprising spirit.

Because of reliance on the MS&L for passage between Hyde Junction and Ashburys where, at the West Junction, Midland freight traffic could diverge to the Midland sidings and goods stations at Ashton Road and Ancoats, and the roundabout nature of the route, the Midland pressed the

MS&L to agree to the construction of a more direct line between Ashburys East Junction and Reddish Junction, as yet unbuilt which the two companies had been empowered to take over from the intended Manchester & Stockport Railway Company by an Act of 24 June 1869. Added to this was a further branch from Reddish Junction, connecting with the MS&L at Romiley Junction to complete the new route.

For this new route from Manchester to Stockport Benton & Woodiwiss were the contractors at a tendered price of £152,197 and use of the line commenced with goods traffic on the section from Romiley Junction to Bredbury Junction on 15 February 1875. Passenger services followed on 1 April, and the further section from Ashburys East Junction to Romiley Junction, bringing into eventual use the stations at Belle Vue (1 September), Reddish (1 December) and Bredbury (1 September), followed for goods on 17 May 1875 and for passengers on 2 August, along with the connecting line from Reddish Junction to Brinnington Junction. On this new route Bredbury station is approached from the Romiley direction by a falling gradient to 1 in 94 as the line to Bredbury Junction falls away at 1 in 71 on the west side. Bredbury tunnels (160 yards) are side by side but on different levels and gradients and only the direct line to Ashburys passes through Bredbury station (179m 34c).

Opposite top
Market Street, Manchester, *c*1903.

Opposite centre
The 'Seven Stars' at Withy Grove, Manchester, 'the oldest licensed house in Great Britain' according to the sign.

Opposite bottom
Delightful period scene in Manchester's Piccadilly with a host of then almost new tramcars and various horse-drawn carriages, 10 October 1903.

Top
Bredbury station (GC & Midland) looking towards Romiley, 8 July 1967. The line on the right at a lower level from Bredbury Junction (CLC) was by then disused.

Centre
Bredbury station, before the rebuilding, looking towards Romiley, 8 July 1967. The station buildings on the 'up' platform were demolished during modernisation.

Bottom
The LNWR Royal Train passing Bredbury behind a pair of finely turned out Midland 4-4-0s, 12 July 1905.

Once a village and part of an urban district of Bredbury and Romiley, two miles north-east of Stockport, Bredbury had a parish population of 4691 at the turn of the century with a variety of dwellings stretching along the road from Stockport to Hyde. The station was modernised in 1976 and platform levels raised, the old main buildings on the New Mills side being demolished and replaced by a new booking hall and office. The original waiting room on the Manchester platform now suffers the indignity of finding itself three steps below platform level, its construction on timber piles set into the side of the embankment mitigating against its being raised. The footbridge, a 1916 addition, remains in use and the smart original stationmaster's house still survives in excellent condition on the right-hand side of the approach road.

GCR services in 1903 comprised eight trains to London Road and one Midland train (the 9.47am) to Victoria whilst in the reverse direction there were eleven trains with a 2.20pm Midland service to Bredbury from Victoria. Today, with the growth of suburbia and the building of new housing estates in the Bredbury area, some thirty-seven trains go to London Road, renamed Piccadilly following electrification, and there are thirty-five in the New Mills direction. On Saturdays there are thirty and twenty-eight, and on Sunday nine and ten trains respectively.

Leaving Bredbury the main line crosses over the Hyde road and the

Top
Bredbury during the hard winter of 1904, with St Marks church on the left.

Centre
The stationmaster's house at Bredbury station which has fortunately survived the modernisation exercise.

Bottom
Bredbury station as modernised with platform levels raised, leaving the 'down' waiting room below platform level! A diesel multiple unit for New Mills stands in the 'up' platform, 29 October 1984.

former Stockport to Woodley line of the CLC with the site of Bredbury Junction on the left, and was then joined by a branch on the right from Lingard's Lane Colliery, which had accommodation sidings adjacent to the signal box of that name. Just beyond this point, a new station, Brinnington, has been constructed one mile north of Bredbury to serve the growing community of (according to BR) some 120,000 living in post-war housing estates in the area. Though not then quite complete the station was opened on 12 December 1977. It comprises two platforms, a modern ticket office and shelters.

Three-quarters of a mile beyond is Reddish Junction (181 miles 4 chains) which brings the GCR & Midland Joint line from Brinnington Junction. Just beyond, the impressive brick-arched Reddish viaduct carries the line over the River Tame and, after passing under the former LNWR line between Stockport and Guide Bridge, Reddish North station is reached (182 miles 12 chains).

Originally opened on 1 December 1875 as Reddish, the station has suffered the depredations of time and the once impressive buildings have now been reduced to a single-storey booking office and waiting room on the 'down' platform, both the original two-storey gable buildings each side – originally a stationmaster's house and a parcels office – having been demolished. The earlier wooden waiting room with a slate roof on the New Mills platform has also gone and has been replaced by a modern utilitarian corrugated-roofed steel sheet-sided 'hutch' with a bench. It became Reddish North on 24 July 1951 and today has a good service in both directions. The goods yard is used by firms making timber-fencing and cement products, with the original goods shed surviving as part of these operations. As with many railway stations a local hostelry is immediately adjacent and 'The Railway', a Whitbread house, stands opposite the station approach.

Top
Reddish viaduct looking south, 23 September 1972.

Centre
Reddish (GC & Midland) station (now Reddish North) 'down' platform buildings, 30 August 1969.

Bottom
Reddish North station from the goods yard looking north, 30 August 1969.

This section of line was later maintained by the Great Central and mileposts are to their design though oddly the mileages given are from Rowsley on the Midland system, and have not been changed into line with the revised Midland system of measuring mileages (to most locations) by the shortest available route from St Pancras.

Passing beneath both the Stockport canal and the former Great Central route from Guide Bridge to Manchester Central, the line curves to the right and enters Belle Vue station (183 miles 32 chains), once busy not only with main line traffic but also with excursions bringing trainloads of pleasure-seekers from all points of the compass to enjoy the delights of Belle Vue Zoological Gardens and Pleasure Grounds.

Established by John Jennison in 1836 the gardens and pleasure grounds at one time covered forty-five acres and had, besides an extensive zoo, flower gardens, two great lakes, rock mazes, conservatories, vineries and fernhouses, a music hall affording 'shelter for ten thousand visitors' and a tea-room seating one thousand was open all day. Additional interests were firework displays and reproductions of Roman architecture, such as 'The Temple of Janus' inside which visitors would be entertained by a 'diaphonic phanopticon' depicting the 'Horrors of War'. In the 1850s and 1860s Longsight (LNWR) was the most conveniently-placed station and excursionists from Derby travelled there via the London & North Western Railway until the opening of the Midland's Belle Vue station on 1 September 1875. A special excursion platform was provided on the 'up' side of the new station.

The glories of Belle Vue have now pased into history and all that remains is the exhibition hall, new housing estates having been built over much of the old grounds.

The station has been modernised by sweeping away the old buildings

Top
Reddish North as it was on 31 October 1984 showing the original footbridge and goods shed beyond. Only the central block of the 'down' station buildings remains.

Centre
Stanier Class 5 4-6-0 on an Ashton Road to Gowhole freight train passing through Reddish North station, 9 June 1965.

Bottom
A deserted Belle Vue station looking towards Manchester, 1 May 1970.

and awnings along with the signal box which stood at the south end of the Manchester platform. All that remains is the original footbridge, minus the section which once led from the overbridge level across to the road on the east side of the station, and a sad solitary platform seat with cast-iron letters, two of which are missing. Modern corrugated-iron-roofed shelters on each platform and a tiny cramped booking office on the 'down' platform at the face of the station approach complete the scene, far removed from the glories of past days. A regular d.m.u. service operates to and from Piccadilly while freight and some express passenger services pass through the station without calling.

Continuing northwards the line curves towards the west and on the right stand the remains of the Midland's former Belle Vue Locomotive Depot and Workshops, opened in 1871 at a cost of £19,000 and then known simply as 'Manchester'. The fitting and repair shops, at the rear of the main square brick 'roundhouse', which had a central 42-foot turntable and radiating lines for the storage and maintenance of locomotives, were extended in 1892 following the installation of a large new coalstage in 1882. A 46-foot turntable was delivered in 1877 and installed outside and in 1899 the turntable in the shed was increased to 55 feet in diameter to cater for larger locomotives. The earlier 0-6-0 tender and tank locomotives were later supplemented by 0-4-4 tank engines for local passenger workings. In 1916 the allocation was one 2-4-0; twelve class 2 4-4-0s; one class 3 4-4-0; nine 0-6-0 tanks; nine class 2, and 28 class 3 0-6-0. goods tender engines. The shed closed on 16 April 1956 and the remaining buildings today serve industrial uses.

The line now curves round to join the MS&L (later Great Central, then LNER line at Ashbury's East Junction to rejoin the earlier route to London Road and by using this route the

Top
Belle Vue station shorn of buildings and canopies, with an 'up' diesel multiple unit for New Mills, 31 October 1984.

Centre
Sole survivor of a once plentiful piece of station furniture at Belle Vue – the humble platform seat – 31 October 1984.

Bottom
Picnic parties in Belle Vue gardens c1930.

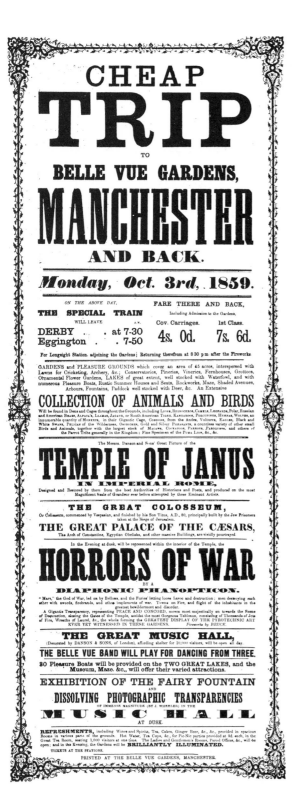

distance from St Pancras to Manchester was shortened by just under two miles to 186 miles 3 chains.

Part 2 – Routes to Manchester Central:

At this juncture it is necessary to explain some detailed history. The Stockport & Woodley Junction Railway was promoted by local interests and by the MS&LR which provided three-fifths of the capital. The latter company also suggested it should work the line and on 15 May 1860 the Act of Incorporation was sealed.

West of Stockport another company, the Stockport, Timperley & Altrincham Junction Railway was promoted to build a line designed to link the S&WJR with the Manchester South Junction and Altrincham at the latter place and at Timperley, and also make a connection with the LNWR system at Broadheath. This railway was authorised by an Act of 22 July 1861 with the Great Northern also becoming financially involved along with the MS&L and they then became the fourth component of the Cheshire Lines Committee.

It was therefore over the former S&WJct and ST&AJR railways that the Midland ran before leaving, via Heaton Mersey East Junction, to join the Manchester South District Railway, the new route adopted from 2 August 1880 into Central station for Midland main-line trains.

This page top
Excursion leaflet for Belle Vue in 1859.

Bottom
The Midland's motive power depot and workshops at Belle Vue in April 1936, with the line from Belle Vue station and the south crossing from the centre distance towards Manchester to the right.

Opposite page top
Stockport Tiviot Dale station buildings in 1962.

Centre
'Jubilee' 4-6-0 45607 *Fiji* arriving in Stockport Tiviot Dale station with the 12.10pm stopping train to Chinley in May 1961.

Bottom
Carved stone decoration set in the station frontage of Tiviot Dale station linking the GN (Great Northern) MS&L (Manchester, Sheffield and Lincolnshire) and M (Midland) railways (now in Stockport Municipal Museum).

The Manchester South District Railway Company was incorporated on 5 August 1873 with a capital of £350,000 to build a line from a junction with the CLC Cornbrook to Cressington line at what became Throstle Nest Junction, to Alderley. A further Act of 30 June 1874 authorised a branch from the Didsbury area to Heaton Mersey to join up with the CLC.

The Midland now became interested in the lines and in 1875 suggested that the portion north of Stockport should become part of the CLC system. Their interest was further intensified by the MS&L giving the Midland three years' notice under agreement to quit the London Road station accommodation by 1 January 1879.

The line, as yet unbuilt, was eventually added to the Sheffield & Midland Joint Committee under the Midland Railway (Further Powers) Act of 11 August 1876, the GNR having dropped out in November 1874, whilst the MS&L could not decide whether or not to support the line but also, in the end, opted out in July 1876, the Midland thereby retaining sole active interest.

By a further Act dated 12 July 1877 the railway became solely vested in the Midland, and a GNR option to become joint owners, not being taken up, expired on 11 August 1878.

The original plans were largely used, the Midland merely remodelling the line to its own requirements. John S. Wilkinson, the original engineer, was instructed to prepare plans, specifications and bills of quantity for letting the works, and the contract went to McGregor & Badman of Darwen, Lancs, for £145,790 13s 1½d with construction beginning in June 1877. The same firm was given the contract for the four stations at a cost of £15,159 13s 9d.

The line opened between Heaton Mersey (later Heaton Mersey East) Junction, just west of Stockport Tiviot Dale station, and Throstle Nest (later Throstle Nest East) Junction on the CLC near Cornbrook on 1 January 1880 with intermediate stations at Heaton Mersey, Didsbury, Withington & Albert Park, and Chorlton-cum-Hardy still unfinished, and a local service was introduced on that date between Manchester Central and Stockport Tiviot Dale, followed on 22 March 1880 by a 'shuttle service' between Central and London Road stations which ran, however, for only

a few years, ceasing on 1 January 1885.

Because of the history of the scheme, the stations were typical of MS&LR and CLC rather than Midland design, even the lamp posts being MS&LR pattern, although signalling, installed at a cost of £3200, was purely Midland. However, soon after opening the line, largely in a cutting north of Heaton Mersey, the Midland was faced with a number of large bills for rebuilding a number of road overbridges which needed reconstruction.

This new route into Manchester Central via Stockport Tiviot Dale served well until the end of the century, when the Midland decided to construct an entirely new and more direct line to the south beyond Heaton Mersey, avoiding any complications with other companies' trains and congestion at various points on the existing route. A new line, the New Mills and Heaton Mersey Railway, was authorised by an Act of 6 August 1897 and two contracts let for its construction. Walter Scott & Company were awarded the southern section, including Disley tunnel, whilst the northern end contract was let to Henry Lovatt.

A short section at the northern end was opened from Heaton Mersey to Cheadle Heath on 1 October 1901 for local passenger services to Manchester Central and the remainder of the route from New Mills to Cheadle Heath, together with the curve to the CLC at Cheadle Junction, opened for

Opposite top left
The huge viaduct which carries the LNWR Crewe to Manchester main line over part of Stockport, the River Mersey and the CLC line.

Opposite top
Teviot Dale West signal box and station staff c1901. The station became Tiviot Dale at a later date.

Opposite centre
Street scene in Stockport market c1896.

Opposite bottom
Street scene in Stockport market with the same attractive glazed market hall on 3 November 1984, almost 90 years later.

This page top
The viaduct at New Mills.

Centre
Newtown Viaduct, New Mills looking east c1904, with the line to New Mills station diverging in the background to the left.

Bottom
LNWR 'Renown' class 4-4-0 5157 *Black Prince* at the head of the 12.55pm Liverpool Central to Chinley express, with through carriages for St Pancras, near Disley tunnel 12 July 1928.

goods traffic on 5 May 1902 and for passengers on 1 July 1902. The new line avoided the steeply-graded and sharply-curved line via Marple and Stockport, with its complications of joint ownership and operation, and at last gave the Midland a fast and direct route into Central station.

Leaving the old route at New Mills South Junction, the new line was to swing to the west and in a little over two miles enter Disley tunnel, second largest on the Midland at 3,866 yards, which penetrates the hillside passing beneath the Peak Forest canal, the townships of Disley and High Lane, and the GC and NS joint line from Macclesfield, before emerging in a deep cutting near Hazel Grove. The tunnel was completed in 1901, its construction being the most expensive work on the line.

Sixty-nine chains beyond the tunnel, Hazel Grove station (177 miles 22 chains), built to serve the local township, opened with the new route on 1 July 1902, a single island platform with an overall canopy and central office block comprising the usual facilities with the station signal box at the eastern end, the 'up' and 'down' lines passing either side of both. There was, however, another station, Hazelgrove, nearby on the LNWR route between Stockport and Whaley Bridge, which served the local popula-

tion and which was more conveniently situated. The Midland station, at which only a few trains called, survived until the middle of the First World War, closing on 1 January 1917.

Construction of this particular stretch of line was costly in view of the many cuttings, embankments and viaducts which were required. A large workforce was necessary and those construction workers involved in the section near Hazel Grove lived in specially-built houses near the 'Rising Sun' public-house. These houses stand today and are still called 'Navvy Mansions'.

Passing over Norbury Viaduct (No. 21) and the aforementioned LNWR line to Whaley Bridge, the Midland line reaches Bramhall Moor Lane Goods depot (178 miles 48 chains) which closed, except for private sidings facilities, on 30 January 1965. Passing beneath both the main LNWR line to Manchester and then the LNWR line from Northenden to Stockport, the Midland reached Cheadle Heath (181 miles 23

Top
The south portal of Disley tunnel showing Midland signal details.

Centre
Hazel Grove Midland station which opened 1 July 1902 and closed 1 January 191

Bottom
London Road, Hazel Grove, looking towards the 'Rising Sun' from near Chapel Street *c*1906.

chains) where the tracks separated
before entering the station so as to
serve four platform faces, of which
the west-side pair, known as the
Liverpool-platforms, gave access via
a curve to Cheadle Junction on the
CLC lines, to Liverpool. However,
by means of crossover roads at the
northern end of the station, trains for
the direct route to Manchester could
use both these platforms and there
was also a bay alongside the 'up'
main platform on the east side at the
southern end. Public access to all
platforms was by an overbridge
connecting from the station buildings
on the east side of the line. The
station opened on 1 October 1901
with local passenger services to and
from Manchester Central.

Cheadle Heath came to be known
as a place 'in its own right' because
early gazeteers frequently described it
as 'a place with a Midland Railway
station, one mile east-north-east of
Cheadle itself and having a post

Top
'Compound' 4-4-0 40929 heads a 'down'
Grand National excursion to Aintree
beween Hazel Grove and Bramhall Moor
Lane, 7 April 1951.

Centre
Group of railway platelayers who were
responsible for maintaining the Midland
line around Hazel Grove, and who worked
from the crossing at Norbury Hollow, are
here captured by the camera *c*1908.

Bottom right
A 'Stanier' 2-8-0 heads towards Bramhall
Moor Lane with a train of 'up' empties
*c*1952.

Bottom left
A leaflet advertising the opening of the
new line between New Mills and Heaton
Mersey on 5 May 1902 for goods and
mineral traffic.

MIDLAND RAILWAY

OPENING OF NEW LINE

BETWEEN

NEW MILLS

AND

HEATON MERSEY

ON MONDAY,

MAY 5th,

The New Line between New Mills and Heaton Mersey
will be opened for

GOODS & MINERAL TRAFFIC. A NEW DEPÔT

HAS BEEN PROVIDED AT

Cheadle Heath,

and one will shortly be opened at

HAZEL GROVE

(BRAMHALL MOOR LANE).

☞ At the depôts named ample accommodation for
dealing with traffic of every description has been provided, including Goods Sheds, Warehouses, Cattle Pens,
Tipping Docks, Stacking Ground for Goods and Coal, &c.

Orders and other communications should be addressed to
Mr. JARVIS, Goods Agent, at Cheadle Heath New Station, or
26, Wellington Road, North, Stockport; to the Station Master at the
Hazel Grove (Bramhall Moor Lane Goods Depôt when opened); or to
Mr. W. E. ADIE, Goods Manager, Derby.

Derby, April, 1902. **JOHN MATHIESON, General Manager.**

MIDLAND RAILWAY

OPENING OF
CHEADLE HEATH STATION
FOR PASSENGER TRAFFIC.

On TUESDAY, OCTOBER 1st, 19__
a New Station will be opened at CHEADLE HEA__
and a Service of Passenger Trains established betwe__

MANCHESTER (CENTR__
AND
CHEADLE HEAT__

ON WEEKDAYS AS FOLLOWS

JOHN MATHIESON, General Man__

Top left
Light and shade – a fine railway study depicting Class 4F 0-6-0 44022 on a 'down' mineral approaching Cheadle Heath, whilst a freight train passes over the Midland line on the LNWR line from Northenden Junction.

Top right
Poster advertising the opening of Cheadle Heath station. The first weekday timetable is shown at the bottom of the poster.

Centre
A view of the almost new carriage and goods sidings at Cheadle Heath captured by the camera in 1904-5.

Bottom
Cheadle Heath station when almost new, looking north, 25 February 1903. The Liverpool platforms are on the left and Manchester platforms to the right.

office with telegraphic services'. Nearby Cheadle was then a busy place with printing and bleaching works, silk and cotton mills and a population of some 9,000.

Cheadle, of course, had its own two railway stations, one on the CLC line from Stockport to West Timperley, and one on the LNWR line from Northenden to Stockport.

When using the new route, passengers for the Stockport area could alight at Cheadle Heath, and the Midland thereby avoided becoming involved in the congestion between New Mills and Romiley aggravated by having to pass through Stockport and also avoided the sharp curves and steep gradients on the old route.

A good initial local service was provided from Cheadle Heath with sixteen trains daily each way, the fastest non-stop reaching Central station in 15 minutes. There was, however, no Sunday service. Expresses from St Pancras now did the trip to Manchester via Cheadle Heath in 3 hours 50 minutes including a 4-minute stop at Leicester, and in 1904 a further 15 minutes was clipped off this time.

Cheadle Heath closed for passengers on 2 January 1967 and to goods on 1 July 1968. Only remains of some of the buildings on the Liverpool platforms survive whilst the Manchester side is cleared away and occupied by two through tracks. Beyond Cheadle Heath the Midland line to Central is dismantled and the route from New Mills is now for freight only, swinging onto the former CLC line to the west via Cheadle Junction.

Leaving Cheadle Heath station, the then new Midland route crossed over both the River Mersey and the CLC lines, Heaton Mersey locomotive depot being on the east side of the line between the CLC line and the river.

Top
A detail of Cheadle Heath station showing water column, station nameboard and lamp post, 25 February 1903.

Centre
Deeley 0-6-4 tank 2008 at Cheadle Heath with an 'up' local c1908.

Bottom
Cheadle Heath station looking south in 1946. Note the station booking office on the bank on the left of the picture and the goods warehouse on the right.

A little further north was Heaton Mersey Station Junction, which took that name with the opening of the new line, standing where the line from Stockport came in from the right to join the main route via a sharp curve with a 15mph speed restriction before running into Heaton Mersey station. Heaton Mersey locomotive depot opened in January 1889 and was a CLC establishment used by both the Midland the Great Central. In early years a couple of Midland 4-4-0s, three or four 0-4-4 tank engines and a number of 0-6-0 tender engines were based there, but with the opening of the new line through Cheadle Heath several new 0-6-0 tanks were provided to work Manchester South District services, superseded later by Deeley 0-6-4 tanks which worked the services until 1934-5, when 2-6-2Ts and 2-6-4Ts arrived, although the latter's stay was brief. The old shed was re-roofed in the 1950s and the depot finally closed on 6 May 1968, the buildings being demolished with no trace now remaining.

Heaton Mersey station (182 miles 29 chains) was opened for passenger traffic on 1 January 1880 and had twenty-one local trains each way daily, a limited number of expresses also calling. It closed to passengers on 3 July 1961 when it lost its services except for the use of the coal depot in the two sidings of the goods yard. Coal drops were built in 1904 for the use of Messrs Melland & Coward whose bleach works, founded by Samuel Oldknow c1786, are nearby on the River Mersey bank. The coal depot continued in use until October 1963 but today no trace of the station remains because of intensive re-development of the area.

Top
LMS 2-6-2 tank 40124 crosses over to the Liverpool lines at Cheadle Heath North Junction with a local train from Manchester Central, 26 July 1952.

Centre
'Jubilee' 4-6-0 45694 *Bellerophon* heads an 'up' express past Cheadle Heath North signal box 1952.

Bottom
The Stockport road at Cheadle Heath – a modern view.

Leaving Heaton Mersey and passing beneath the LNWR line from Wilmslow to London Road, the Midland continued down a falling gradient of 1 in 160 easing to 1 in 120 into Didsbury station (183 miles 43 chains). This was formerly a place of detached residences and wide-open spaces where the Manchester wool and cotton merchants lived out their detached existences, away from the smoke and grime, squalor and poverty of the poorer suburbs closer to the city centre where workpeople inhabited more humble abodes. At the turn of the century the population of Didsbury was over 9,000.

Most of the original road bridges over the railway consist of cast-iron main support beams made by R.&.C.(J) Rankin & Company of Liverpool, with brick-arch infils and stone-topped brick parapets; but the bridge at the north end of Didsbury station, and the second bridge south

Top
The bridge carrying the Midland main line over both the Cheshire Lines and the River Mersey, looking south towards Cheadle Heath.

Centre
LMS 2-6-2 tank 40093 crossing the Mersey with a local train for Manchester Central in 1950s.

Bottom
Heaton Mersey station looking south *c*1920, with the station staff posed between trains.

of the later bridge built to carry the LNWR Wilmslow-Levenshulme line (opened 1 May 1909) over the Midland, are of a different iron-girder construction with intermediate decking.

Didsbury station opened with the line on 1 January 1880 although some work still remained to be completed. It had a platform each side of the double track main line connected by an overbridge, and the goods yard and signal box were to the south of the station, beyond the School Lane overbridge, on the 'down' (west) side of the line with a lay-by siding on the 'up' side. The station was actually situated at Barlow Moor, a small village about half-a-mile north of the old centre of Didsbury. A horse-and-carriage dock siding was added in 1881 and end screens were provided to the platform awnings in August 1883 by Chadwick & Company.

Didsbury, like Withington, once had a bookstall on the 'down' platform beneath its footbridge, but this was subsequently re-sited in the booking hall, thus removing a small problem for late evening travellers from town for the stations were so very similar that it was not unknown for passengers to alight at the wrong place! It had a regular service of trains in each direction and two 'up' London expresses stopped in the morning with a similar return facility being provided in the evenings. Other regular traffic included milk vans dropped off daily for Heald's Dairy and later conveyed south when empty.

Opposite top right
'Stanier' Class 5 4-6-0 44986, with self-weighing tender, on an 'up' passenger leaving Heaton Mersey in the early 1950s past Heaton Mersey Station junction box. Beyond the box the line to Stockport diverges to the left.

Opposite centre
BR 'Standard' Class 4 2-6-0 76089 enters Heaton Mersey in July 1961 with the 1.30pm Manchester Central to Sheffield stopping train.

Opposite bottom
Didsbury Road, Heaton Moor, which lies to the west of the Midland line, is depicted in this interesting period scene.

This page top
'Jubilee' 4-6-0 45604 *Ceylon* on the 9.00am Manchester Central to St Pancras express passes Class 5 4-6-0 44664 on a 'down' stopping train near Didsbury in 1953.

Centre
Class 5 4-6-0 44861 heads a 'down' express between Heaton Mersey and Didsbury *c*1953.

Bottom
A Deeley 0-6-4 tank enters Didsbury with an 'up' local train *c*1908.

Didsbury station closed on 2 January 1967, goods traffic having earlier ceased on 2 November 1964. Today the local population is served by East Didsbury and Burnage station on the old LNWR line from Alderley Edge which terminates in Piccadilly station. Since closure, Didsbury station was, for a time, used by a hardware dealer but has now been demolished though platform faces remain, gradually being obliterated by a vigorous growth of small trees and bushes. The perimeter and lower part of the booking office walls and, in the forecourt, a clock tower and drinking fountain, remain, the latter dedicated to the memory of Dr J. Wilson Rhodes, a philanthropist (1847-1909) whom the legend describes as 'A Friend to Humanity'.

A little further north was Withington and Albert Park station (184 miles 16 chains) originally named Withington but re-named from August 1884's timetable. Following further development it was re-named Withington and West Didsbury from 1 April 1915 (1 December 1914 according to Railway Clearing House records), 'Albert Park' being deleted. Only a single boundary wall, to the left of the station approach road off Lapwing Lane, now remains and the site is occupied by Brankgate Court, a modern block of flats.

Immediately opposite the station approach Old Lansdowne Road leads

into the heart of the Albert Park housing estate. This exclusive residential district was developed in the mid-1860s with the construction of Palatine Road from Withington to Northenden and was further developed in the 1880s following the arrival of the railway. The estate was named after the Queen's Consort, a second estate named Victoria Park being developed concurrently some distance away and nearer to the city centre, with a further district, Alexandra Park, to the west.

An urban district only four miles from Central station, Withington was another favoured residential area, with many fine villas and other suburban residences and the 'Lancashire Independent College' was situated there. In the year 1900 the parish had a population of 16,000 and the wider urban district increased that total to over 36,000.

Beyond Withington the line continued almost straight for 1½ miles, the MS&L (Great Central) line from Guide Bridge joining from the right at Chorlton Junction, and then ran, on what was to become CLC Chorlton Branch metals, into Chorlton-cum-Hardy station (186 miles 6 chains).

Serving a population of several thousand, the station opened with the line on 1 January 1880 as part of the Midland's Manchester South District route but on 1 October 1891 ownership was transferred to the Cheshire Lines Committee coincident with the opening of the Great Central's Fallowfield line. Station accommodation comprised a double-gabled red-brick main building on the 'down' platform with the later addition of a commodious glass-roofed wooden shelter on the 'up' side. A new awning was provided to the northbound platform in 1884-5 for which Mr W. Brown received nearly £950 and R. Neil & Sons provided 'up'-side coverings in 1892 for the sum of £1,442. A large goods yard was provided beyond the north end of the 'down' platform, with a Midland-style signal box opposite, on the 'up' side, later replaced by one of CLC design.

Top
Didsbury station looking towards Heaton Mersey, 8 July 1967.

Centre
Exterior of Didsbury station, 8 July 1967.

Bottom
Didsbury village main street as it was in 1902 with horse-drawn vehicles still in the ascendancy!

Initially, in addition to local trains, four or five main-line trains called. 'Up' and 'down' slow trains between the south and Manchester continued to call there until the station closed on 2 January 1967, goods traffic having ceased, apart from private sidings, on 30 November 1964. By May 1969 the station buildings had been demolished.

The final stretch of line continues for a further 1½ miles, passing through a cutting and then the 92-yard Throstle Nest South tunnel, which carried the line beneath the Manchester South Junction & Altrincham Railway line just west of its Old Trafford station, and then the 224-yard Throstle Nest North tunnel (which was reduced to 115 yards following the building of the south to west curve). It then swings to the right and joints the CLC main line from Liverpool at Throstle Nest (East) Junction (187 miles 57 chains) over a curve on which a 20mph restriction was enforced.

To the right was the Cornbrook locomotive depot comprising a three-road shed and turntable, squeezed in between the running lines and the Bridgewater canal. Here the Midland housed and serviced its locomotives until the opening of the CLC shed at Trafford Park in March 1895. In 1880 Cornbrook had two 2-4-0 and thirteen 4-4-0 tender engines (with a further two 4-4-0s available, but nominally at the Belle Vue depot), and nine 0-4-4 tank engines. The later twenty-road locomotive depot at Trafford Park initially had part of its accommodation on the southern side allocated to the Midland, with their initials over the doorways of the appropriate roads, and in addition had its own turntable, coal stage and offices. From here 0-6-0 tanks, later replaced by Deeley 0-6-4 tanks, worked local passenger services, while a dozen or so Johnson 4-4-0s worked long-distance trains, later supplanted by Compound 4-4-0s and,

Top
A 2183 Class 4-4-0 on an 'up' express between Withington and Didsbury just before the turn of the century.

Centre
1532 series Midland 0-4-4 tank heads a 'down' local into Withington and Albert Park station.

Bottom
A business train entering what was by then Withington and West Didsbury station *c*1920. The platform is thronged with passengers going up to town.

in LMS days, Stanier Class 5 and 'Jubilee' 4-6-0s. The shed closed on 4 March 1968 and the site is now occupied by a freightliner depot.

Beyond Cornbrook East and West Junctions the line ran along the gently-curving Manchester viaduct, almost a mile in length, past the spurs to the GNR's Deansgate Goods depot and the CLC's Goods depot, both of which lay to the left, and then by means of a sharp left-hand curve entered Central station with its magnificent arched single-span glass and iron roof.

According to Midland Board Minutes the train shed was built of steel because of its comparatively low cost in the year 1877, and was erected by Andrew Handyside & Company of Derby and London with a contract of £58,032 13s 1d. The single-span roof is 210 feet wide and 550 feet long, with sixteen steel arches along its length and is covered with 125,000 square feet of slate, glass and wood weighing in all some 2,400 tons. The engineers for the project, on behalf of the GNR, Midland, and MS&L companies (Cheshire Lines Committee) were Richard Johnson, Andrew Johnston and Charles Sacré respectively. Robert Neill and Sons of Manchester were responsible for the sub-structure of the station up to platform level at a cost of £124,778 under a contract let in October 1875. Masonry infill was not, however, as cheap as steel and the huge 'temporary' facade erected at the end of the train shed lasted, in fact, for the whole of the station's life until closure on 5 May 1969.

A plan to build an hotel as part of the station buildings never materialised but the Midland built its own magnificent hotel in 1903 on a site which fronted on to Peter Street, its rear being opposite to Central station.

William Towle, the Midland Hotels' Manager, saw potential for a new hotel of high standard since

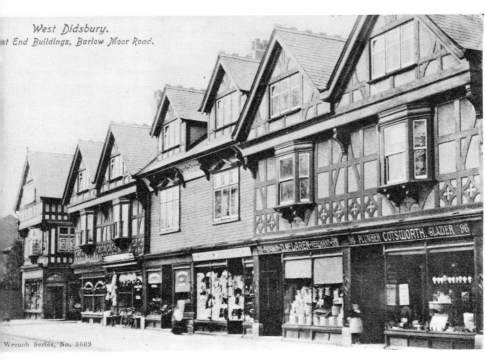

Top
Johnson 4-4-0 1336 at the head of a train of arc-roofed stock at Withington and Albert Park station *c*1890.

Centre
The entrance to Withington and Albert Park station – nothing in this view now remains except a section of the wall to the left.

Bottom
West End Buildings – a typical row of small shops but architecturally rather attractive – at Barlow Moor Road, West Didsbury. Traders include a butcher, a ladies outfitter, a provision merchant (or grocer), and a plumber and glazier.

Manchester could not, at that time, offer such a facility. The Midland's architect, Charles Trubshaw, set to work on plans for the building to be erected which, in 1896, cost £365,000. Main objections came from Charles Heywood, owner of the 'Gentlemen's Concert Hall' which had been erected by private subscription in 1831 and where Charles Hallé had made his first appearance and later founded the now world-famous orchestra. Heywood finally agreed to sell on condition that the Midland incorporated a 'theatre-cum-concert hall' within their new hotel.

Trubshaw's design for a six-storey steel-framed building, with elaborate decor, carefully filtered air-conditioning system, elaborate fireproofing and a wide range of special facilities, was to cost the Midland £1¼ million and was eventually opened on 5 September 1903 when its directors gave a dinner for special guests. There were French and German restaurants, a Grill Room, Billiards and Smoking Rooms (a male preserve), a Turkish Bath, a Tailor's Shop, a Chemist, a Post Office and, for the ladies, a Parisian Milliner's Shop. Tea or coffee could be taken in the Winter Gardens on the hotel roof where, to musical accompaniment, one could view the city stretched out below.

An 800-seat theatre, with an entrance facing Central station, frequently hosted such stars as Edward Terry, Mrs Patrick Campbell, and Harry Pellisier and his Follies. The theatre curtain fell for the final time in 1922.

Over the years many alterations have taken place, particularly in 1936 when a modern lounge was created in which Henry Hall entertained as a stand-in pianist before becoming the hotel's first musical director, and later still becoming nationally famous as a bandleader with his 'Guest Night' programmes for the BBC.

Top
Class 4F 0-6-0 44332 heads a Manchester express past Chorlton Junction, 28 March 1959.

Centre
A Derby to Manchester stopping train near Chorlton-cum-Hardy hauled by Midland 4-4-0 726.

Bottom
Chorlton-cum-Hardy station on Sunday, 1 January 1967, as a 'down' diesel railcar calls on the last day of passenger services. The station closed to passenger traffic from the following day.

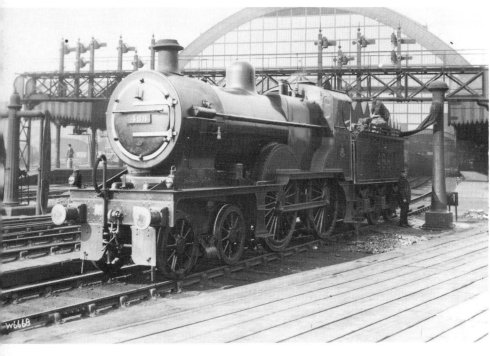

Another historic event at the hotel was the first meeting in May 1904 of the Hon Charles Stewart Rolls and Frederick Henry Royce which resulted in the formation of the world-famous Rolls-Royce Company. A plaque in the hotel marks the occasion. Part of the hotel is today leased as a casino but most of it remains, albeit much modernised, as a tribute to Midland flair and business enterprise.

There was an earlier station, a little to the west of the new Central station, which opened as a temporary terminus on 9 July 1877 and it was into this that the Midland's South District services first ran before the opening of the permanent station on 1 July 1880. The earlier station closed on that date to re-open on 1 December 1880 as Manchester Central Goods, remaining as such until closure on 7 September 1964. Central station originally had seven platforms, two of these being separated by a horse-cab rank. An extra platform was commenced at the end of 1904 on the Lower Mosley Street side of the station and was opened on 1 April 1906 at a cost of some £10,000.

In addition to the South District services, the Midland used Central station for the majority of its services to places south and east of Manchester. London was well served by fast and semi-fast weekday services, the best trains in the 1880s being the 12noon and 4pm, the latter conveying Pullman Parlour Cars, in a best time to St Pancras of 4 hours 15 minutes.

A further Pullman Parlour service ran in the 1880s at 10.10am and a dining saloon-car train ran at 5.15pm, whilst a Pullman sleeping-car train ran to London at 11.50pm, arriving in St Pancras at 5.15am. Nine trains were available to London each day (forming seven actual arrivals) with two on Sundays. Services to other destinations in 1887 included those to Liverpool, Buxton (changing at Millers Dale) and Derby, with some through carriages to Bristol.

Top
Chorlton-cum-Hardy 'down' side station buildings.

Centre
Manchester Central station frontage *c*1911.

Bottom
Midland 4-4-0 488 of Derby shed takes on water at Manchester Central. Note the water deflector plates to prevent axlebox lubrication problems when a pilot engine picked up water.

By the year 1962 'The Palatine', the best regular express, was leaving Central at 2.25pm and reaching St Pancras 3 hours 55 minutes later, at 6.20pm, with stops at Chinley, Miller's Dale, Matlock, Derby and Leicester. This was bettered for a number of years by the Midland Pullman service of the early 1960s which covered the distance in 3 hours 15 minutes, stopping only at Cheadle Heath, this being achieved by a diesel-electric power-car-hauled de luxe Pullman train built by Metro-Cammell. Introduced as a stop-gap measure to provide a high-speed businessmen's service during the electrification of the West Coast main line, it made its last run on 15 April 1966.

Top left
William Towle, the Midland's Hotels Manager, pictured in the garden tea rooms of the Midland Hotel, Manchester, in January 1908.

Top right
The splendid Octagon Lounge of the Midland Hotel, so called because of its eight-sided shape.

Centre
Exterior view of the Midland Hotel at Manchester – a magnificent and impressive addition to the city's accommodation.

Bottom
Tea and music on the roof of the Midland Hotel in its early years – or could it be that the man in the flat cap is on his way to a Hallé Orchestra rehearsal!

Local services on the through route via Bakewell to Manchester Central finally ceased on 6 March 1967, the last local services over the Manchester South District Line to Stockport (Tiviot Dale) having run on Sunday, 1 January 1967. The final local train to Cheadle Heath had run the previous day, this being the 12.48 hauled by Stanier Class 5 4-6-0 44830 inappropriately hauling a set of green SR corridor stock!

Sheffield to Manchester trains were diverted to Piccadilly station from 2 January 1967 but express trains from and to St Pancras and Nottingham

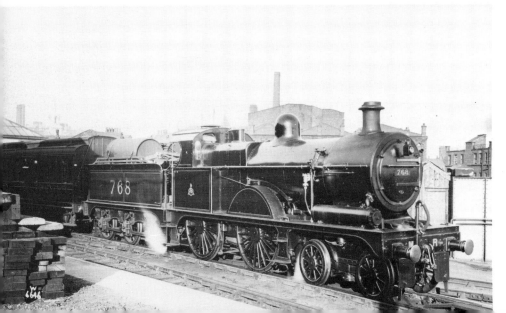

Top
A Midland 4-4-0 (possibly 1744) stands at the head of a special train at Manchester Central *c*1900. It is possibly a special run in connection with the official opening of the N Mills to Heaton Mersey line on 1 July 1902.

Centre
An early view of Manchester Central station from an illustrated catalogue of Messrs Andrew Handyside & Co Ltd, who were responsible for the iron and steel work

Bottom
Immaculate Midland Class 4 Belpaire 4-4-0 768 with Great Eastern type oil-burning apparatus stands at Manchester Central ready to depart with a stopping passenger train for Derby in 1919.

continued to run to and from
Manchester Central using the Matlock
route until 1 January 1968, when they
were also moved to Manchester
(Piccadilly) except for one 'up' night
train which ran from Manchester
Victoria. These trains were diverted
via Chesterfield from 1 July 1968 and
all passenger services between
Ambergate and Chinley via Matlock
were withdrawn on and from
that date.

Central survived for two more years
served by other surviving local
passenger traffic and two 'Sundays
only' expresses on their way from
Liverpool (Lime Street) to Sheffield
(Midland) which were diverted to run
via Oxford Road and Piccadilly
stations, when final closure came from
5 May 1969, the last trains having
actually run between Cheadle Heath
North Junction and Chorlton Junction
on Sunday, 27 April 1969.

The station, now shorn of most of
its railway impedimenta, still stands
today as a tribute to Victorian
engineering skills and is due to
become an exhibition hall.

A retired Great Central clerk, now
in his eighties, and who once worked
at Central Station, was recently asked
for his memories of the Midland.
After a brief pause he replied: 'The
Midland was in a class of its own.' And
so it was.

The memories of the glorious
Midland route through Monsal Dale
and Miller's Dale, now abandoned,
are still sharp (though fading) for
those who were privileged to travel
over that route and, whilst the line
from Cheadle Heath into Manchester
Central is no more, the Dore and
Chinley line survives to provide
today's rail traveller with an
opportunity to travel along it and
marvel at the achievement of our
Victorian forefathers, who carved out
a path for the railway through some of
the most difficult terrain in the country
in order to establish these routes for
the Midland through the Peak.

Top
The interior of Manchester Central as seen
from the catwalk, 23 April 1959.

Centre
Manchester Central as Class 5 4-6-0 44888
waits to depart with the 5.22pm to Buxton,
5 August 1966.

Bottom
Tailpiece photograph – Manchester
Central, in the summer of 1911 with
Midland 'Compound' 4-4-0 1011 making a
stirring departure for London St Pancras.

143

LIST OF STATIONS etc.

Original station name (and company in italics if not MR)	Shortest distance from St Pancras		Officially opened for passenger traffic	Officially closed for passenger traffic from
	miles	chains		
Derby (1st station) (*MCR*)	★		4 June 1839	11 May 1840
Derby (2nd station) (*NMR*)	128	37	11 May 1840	—
Derby, Nottingham Road	128	49	1 September 1856	6 March 1967
Duffield (1st station) (*NMR*)	★		11 May 1840	1 October 1867
Duffield (2nd station)	133	8	1 October 1867	—
Duffield (Wirksworth branch platform)	133	8	1 October 1867	*16 June 1947
Hazelwood	134	77	1 October 1867	*16 June 1947
Shottle	136	43	1 October 1867	*16 June 1947
Idridgehay	138	5	1 October 1867	*16 June 1947
Wirksworth	141	37	1 October 1867	*16 June 1947
Belper (1st station) (*NMR*)	134	79	11 May 1840	10 March 1878
Belper (2nd station)	135	53	10 March 1878	—
Amber Gate (1st station) (*NMR*)	138	18	11 May 1840	1 June 1863
Ambergate (2nd station)	138	1	1 June 1863	10 December 1876
Ambergate (3rd station)	see below			
Wingfield (*NMR*)	141	11	11 May 1840	2 January 1967
Smithy Moor (later Stretton) (*NMR*)	144	30	1 June 1841	11 September 1961
Clay Cross (*NMR*)	142	19	11 May 1840	2 January 1967
Chesterfield (1st station) (*NMR*)	146	15	11 May 1840	2 May 1870
(2nd station)	146	20	2 May 1870	
†Sheepbridge	147	77	1 August 1870	2 January 1967
Unston (later Unstone)	150	14	1 February 1870	29 October 1951
Dronfield	151	14	1 February 1870 re-opened 5 January 1981	2 January 1967
Grindleford	158	69	1 June 1894	—
Hathersage	160	60	1 June 1894	—
Bamford	162	42	1 June 1894	—
Hope	164	25	1 June 1894	—
Edale	169	14	1 June 1894	—
Ambergate (3rd station)	138	18	10 December 1876	—
Watstandwell Bridge (1st station)	140	34	1853	11 November 1894
Whatstandwell Bridge (2nd station)	140	13	11 November 1894	—
Cromford Bridge (*MBM&MJR*)	143	10	20 August 1849	—
Matlock Bath (*MBM&MJR*)	143	73	20 August 1849 re-opened 27 May 1972	6 March 1967
Matlock Bridge (*MBM&MJR*)	145	0	20 August 1849	—
Darley (*MBM&MJR*)	147	14	20 August 1849	6 March 1967
Rowsley (1st station) (*MBM&MJR*)	149	38	20 August 1849	1 August 1862
Rowsley (2nd station)	149	36	1 August 1862	6 March 1967
Bakewell	152	64	1 August 1862	6 March 1967
Hassop	153	65	1 August 1862	17 August 1942
Longstone	155	13	1 June 1863	10 September 1962
Monsal Dale	156	46	1 September 1866	10 August 1959
Millers Dale	159	21	1 June 1863	6 March 1967
Blackwell Mill (halt)	★		before 1910	12 June 1966
Buxton	164	55	1 June 1863	6 March 1967
Peak Forest	163	66	1 February 1867	6 March 1967
Chapel-en-le-Frith	167	42	1 February 1867	6 March 1967
Chinley (1st station)	169	31	1 February 1867	1 June 1902
Chinley (2nd station)	169	39	1 June 1902	—
Bugsworth	170	35	1 February 1867	15 September 1958
New Mills (*MNM&HJ*)	173	15	1 July 1865	
Birch Vale (*MS&L*)	174	73	May 1868	5 January 1970
Hayfield (*MS&L*)	175	69	1 March 1868	5 January 1970
Strines (*MNM&HJ*)	174	48	August 1866(t.t.)	—
Marple (*MS&L*)	176	57	5 August 1862	—
Romiley (*MS&L*)	178	28	5 August 1862	—
Woodley (*MS&L*)	179	46	5 August 1862	—
Hyde (*MS&L*)	181	8	1 March 1858	—
Hyde Junction (*MS&L*)	182	5	February 1863	—
Manchester (Store Street) (*SA&M and M&B*)	187	74	10 May 1842	—
via Guide Bridge				
(later London Road and now Piccadilly)				
	186	3	(*SA&M* use began on 2 June 1843)	
via Belle Vue				
Bredbury (*S&MC*)	179	34	1 September 1875	—
Brinnington (*BR*)	180	35	12 December 1977	—
Reddish (*S&MC*)	182	12	1 December 1875	—
Belle Vue (*S&MC*)	183	32	1 September 1875	—
Stockport (Teviot Dale) (*CLC*)	181	47	1 December 1865	2 January 1967
Heaton Mersey	182	29	1 January 1880	3 July 1961
Didsbury	183	43	1 January 1880	2 January 1967
Withington	184	16	1 January 1880	3 July 1961
Chorlton-cum-Hardy	186	6	1 January 1880	2 January 1967
Manchester Central (1st station) (*CLC*)	189	20	9 July 1877	30 June 1880
Manchester Central (2nd station) (*CLC*)	189	18	1 July 1880	4 May 1969
Hazel Grove	177	22	1 July 1902	1 January 1917
Cheadle Heath	181	23	1 October 1901	2 January 1967

★ Note: The branch was not finally permanently closed to passenger traffic until 1 January 1949
† Renamed Sheepbridge and Whittington Moor reverting to Sheepbridge later

All distances are taken from the official Midland Railway Distance Diagrams except for Brinnington.
Consequent upon the closure of the through route via Bakewell the mileages from St. Pancras by the shortest route via the Dore and Chinley line is now increased by 5 miles and 20 chains for stations beyond and including Chinley.
In all cases the dates of opening refer to the first station on the site and the first station name used is the one quoted.
Entries marked thus ★ indicate where information is lacking.   t.t. = first timetable entry.
Special Note: The mileages in brackets thus: (169 miles 17 chains) give the distance from St Pancras Station, London by the shortest route in accordance with the Midland Railway Distance Diagram Book.

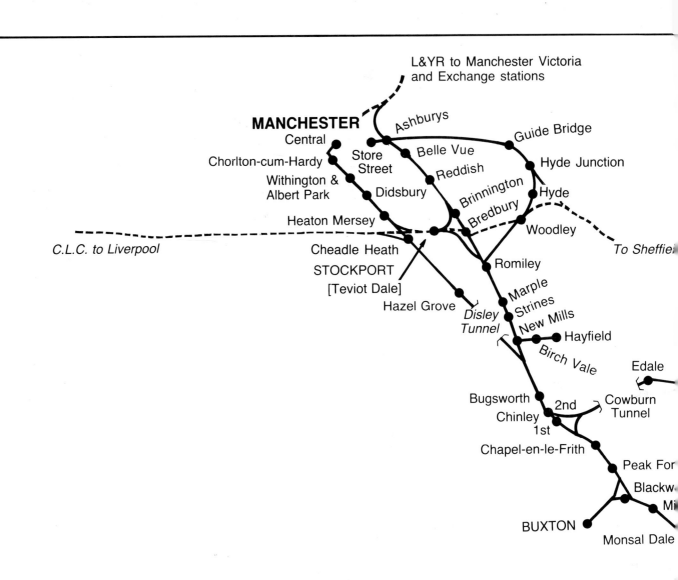

L&YR to Manchester Victoria and Exchange stations

MANCHESTER
Central

Chorlton-cum-Hardy

Withington & Albert Park

Store Street

Ashburys

Belle Vue

Reddish

Guide Bridge

Hyde Junction

Didsbury

Brinnington

Hyde

Heaton Mersey

Bredbury

Woodley

C.L.C. to Liverpool

Cheadle Heath

Romiley

To Sheffie...

STOCKPORT
[Teviot Dale]

Marple

Hazel Grove

Strines

Disley Tunnel

New Mills

Hayfield

Birch Vale

Edale

Bugsworth

2nd

Cowburn Tunnel

Chinley

1st

Chapel-en-le-Frith

Peak For...

Blackw...

M...

BUXTON

Monsal Dale

MIDLAND